"Enchanting, mournful yet hopeful...Childs ruminates almost poetically on the ageless use of stellar navigation by all manner of species, from birds to grasshoppers to great human civilizations, and what happens to them when the stars disappear."

—*BOOKLIST* (starred review)

"By slowly cycling into ever-deeper physical darkness and reconnecting with both the ancient and the surprisingly recent past, Childs shows how a lack of artificial light is not something to fear, but a state of being vital to our biology and our psychology. *The Wild Dark* illuminates all that humanity stands to lose by extinguishing the wondrous, all-encompassing nightscape that is our birthright."

—REBECCA BOYLE, *Our Moon*

"A celebration of the night sky, a testament to how many people are disconnected from the darkness where the stars—used by our ancestors for navigation—shine brilliantly."

—REBECCA SOLNIT, *Hope in the Dark*

"With Childs leading the way, we're never off-course in this cosmic overworld adventure—Dante's Virgil doesn't hold a candle. You'll get thirsty, scraped, and saddle sore. You'll jump at the burst of ordnance and shiver as night creatures slither past. But you'll never again see that big black bowl of night sky as a distant, indifferent void. Nor will you think of it as the realm of gods. You'll no longer take for granted what's being lost to so much bright artifice, the piece of our humanity that's snuffed with it. Once this book has had its way with you, you'll throw down your bag, ditch the headlamp, and turn off that damn phone. You'll revert to the thing we were meant to be—wide-eyed and wild, to the bone."

—AMY IRVINE, *Desert Cabal*

"*The Wild Dark* is a personal journey and a fact-packed thought-provoker."

—JOHAN EKLÖF, *The Darkness Manifesto*

"The firsthand experience of day turning into night, of the quiet, solitude, and beauty that depends on darkness, has become inaccessible to many and forgotten by even more. And why would this matter? What do we lose when we no longer experience a natural night? In *The Wild Dark*, Childs offers a compelling answer, mixing science and history with a journey made of good humor and vibrant language. This is a great read—one that takes the reader on a two-wheeled trek—into the desert, into the dark, under the stars—and shows us what can happen when we pay attention to the ancient wild world that still revolves around us, awaiting our gaze, welcoming our awe, inspiring our praise."

—PAUL BOGARD, *The End of Night*

"As ever, Childs weaves in urgent issues, from what artificial light does to birds, to night sky advocacy, to solutions for protecting the flickering stars that grace us. One leaves this gorgeous book filled with wonder, not only for stars, but for everything from tarantulas to archeoastronomy."

—LAURA PRITCHETT, *Playing with Wildfire*

"With resonant prose and a deep awareness, Childs basks in the awesome wonder of the night sky and reminds us all to do the most intrinsic thing: look up!"

—EVAN SCHERTZ, Maria's Bookshop

"The night sky—the stars and the deep, black spaces between them—may be the source of a particular wild wisdom that throughout our evolutionary history guaranteed our success as a species. Childs has written *The Wild Dark* because we need that vast wisdom now."

—BROOKE WILLIAMS, *Encountering Dragonfly*

"Childs threads celestial connections across time and into space like no other, taking us with him and his compatriots as they travel through the landscape into darkness to reveal the sky's light. The cosmological journey animates the physical one across the desert, and we once again experience the magic in Craig's ability to illuminate our lives through exploring our past. If you've ever stared at the stars and wondered at who or what else had done the same, this book is for you."

—DAVID EVERITT, Back of Beyond Books

"Eyes wide and sparkling with stars, Childs once again takes us on a journey we didn't know we needed—this time into the diminishing darkness of our night skies. With his signature reverence for mystery, adventure, wonder and all things ancient and new, Childs turns scientific inquiry, observational acumen, poetic imagination, and a love of language into a dazzling and tragic image of ourselves—a people so in love with light we are killing the dark. And yet, at every turn, we are also given a reason to laugh, a reason to love, and a reason to pay attention to the marvels that surround us every day. At the heart of this book is a way forward, a reminder of our shared humanity, and a mirror as big as the moon."

—WENDY VIDELOCK, *Wise to the West*

"Join Childs on a rapturous bike adventure, traversing a beautifully crafted narrative that takes you from our electric inferno to the furthest outlook of the nearest heavens."

—MARK SUNDEEN, *Delusions + Grandeur*

"Childs may be best known for looking down and beyond. He has scoured desert floors for signs of moisture in some of the driest places on Earth. He has peered out from a sand burial, a place of respite in the midday blazing heat. And he has carefully scanned canyon alcoves for signs of the ancient ones. In *The Wild Dark*, Childs heads out on two wheels, pedaling away from a place so bright it's clearly visible from space, while searching for the increasing darkness above. 'There has never been this much light,' he writes, as he guides us in an exploration of the night sky in its evolving phases of darkness. He goes deep into the cosmos and into humanity's grasp of the heavens above, as well as the light from below. Despite the complexity, Childs has a simple message: DO look up, where wonder and stories abound."

—HOWARD BERKES,
retired investigations correspondent for NPR

"In a riveting masterpiece of creative nonfiction, author Craig Childs lifts the essential scientific language about light pollution into an absorbing narrative of adventure, meditation and multicultural exploration of human purpose and meaning."

—LES ROKA, *The Utah Review*

THE WILD DARK

The Wild Dark

FINDING THE NIGHT SKY IN THE AGE OF LIGHT

Craig Childs

TORREY HOUSE PRESS

Salt Lake City • Torrey

First Torrey House Press Edition, May 2025
Copyright © 2025 by Craig Childs

Published by Torrey House Press
Salt Lake City, Utah
www.torreyhouse.org

International Standard Book Number: 979-8-89092-018-8
E-book ISBN: 979-8-89092-019-5
Library of Congress Control Number: 2024944827

Cover art by Jeremy Collins
Cover design by Kathleen Metcalf
Interior design by Gray Buck-Cockayne
Distributed to the trade by Consortium Book Sales and Distribution

Torrey House Press offices in Salt Lake City sit on the homelands of Ute, Goshute, Shoshone, and Paiute nations. Offices in Torrey are on the homelands of Southern Paiute, Ute, and Navajo nations.

for Viviana
born of thunder

Contents

At the distance of a star something happened,
and everything began.

—N. Scott Momaday

INTRODUCTION

Night comes slowly. Dusk shakes out its soft, furry tail, and stars appear. The first you'll see is probably not a star but a planet, and you'd want to know what's being wished upon, if it's a dying blue giant several hundred light-years away or a red, dusty ball of rock one orbit out from our own. After the first one or two planets, the next needle pricks will be true stars, their abundance depending on the phase and brightness of the moon and the haze of ambient light. In the rowdy glamour of Las Vegas, if you look closely, three or four will scratch the surface. A little darker and you get hundreds of stars, Betelgeuse hanging between casinos like the red eye of a cyclops in a cave seven hundred light-years deep, or the glimmering blue-white binary of Sirius eight and a half light-years away. A little darker and you get hundreds of stars, and darker than that, thousands. Under full night conditions, a total of nine thousand stars are known to be visible to the unaided eye from around the entire Earth, a few thousand in a single scan from wherever you happen to be.

Do you remember being stopped cold by a brilliant night, seeing more of the heavens than you could rightly address? Was it in a wilderness where the Milky Way is so bright it cast a shadow? A back deck or a porch, rocking chair, dirt road you're rambling along late in the evening, your face turning up to take it all in? It's becoming rarer you might have noticed. When was the last time?

My first time was foisted on me. I must have been five or six and it was somewhere in Colorado because we lived in Denver back then. An hour or two by car out of the city had some wild places and still does today, dirt roads and empty country with no lights. My mom's boyfriend drove a white Dodge pickup and we took it up to the mountains to camp. He was a meaty, kindhearted hockey player from Saskatoon who hauled a full-size mattress in the bed of his truck, and when we got to where we were going, he pulled it out with his big hands and threw it down with a mighty *thwump*. The ground was covered in needles fallen from ponderosa pines, amber and slick. As light faded, trunks of trees stepped farther and farther back and vanished. My mom had brought blankets, a lot of them, and she tucked me in so she and her sweetie could slip away to do whatever adults did, hand in hand in moonless dark. I lay frozen on the mattress, terrified. Perhaps I squeaked a complaint, but I probably stayed quiet, frozen, hearing nothing, not even crickets in chilly mountain air. Under the blankets, I could barely move.

I can't say whether I've had more or less trauma than most. My early years were fine and loving as I recall, but at that moment on the mattress panic was loud, my heart beating in my ears. The dark seemed malevolent, or worse, it felt like nothing at all, no mom out there, no boyfriend, no pickup. I'd fallen from the well and brightly lit world with my eyes darting for anything to grasp. I landed on what was most obvious, a black ring of pines holding a circle above me, a window onto a color I still search to name, *sapphires on silk*. The Milky Way flowed like an event, a splash of paint a hundred thousand light-years across. I knew nothing of light-years, and if I knew of stars it was from nursery rhymes. I'd seen them before, but not to my memory and not eye to eye, not in a way I recognized.

As I looked into the thick of the sky, the weight of the blankets seemed to lift, and a monster was no longer seated on my chest. I won't pretend to remember in detail what I thought that night, but I was acutely aware for the first time of visual infinity, and it was not empty as one might fear. It was chock-full, so busy my eye didn't know where to settle. If I could have reached a hand out from under my blankets—and maybe I did—I would have waved a five-fingered blackness against the sky. I no longer felt alone. How could I? What should have been a complete void was not. My heart settled, breathing slowed. The celestial sphere seemed to sing me off the ledge.

This is how I came to trust the night sky. It's where I still turn when my heart races in the dark and I have to get up from bed and walk outside bare-shouldered, standing with arms folded across my chest as the color of lilac rains down on my skin.

Not everyone feels this way. A friend gets the willies from seeing too many stars at once. Adverse, irrational reactions to seeing outer space are termed *cosmophobia* or *astrophobia*. Space dread. I don't find this an unreasonable response, not if you consider we live on a planet as blood-pumping gut sacks with eyes sophisticated enough to see the cosmos.

Sitting around a campfire in Utah under a Bortle 1 sky—a rating for the darkest sky a person can encounter from the face of the Earth—my friend told me he looks up and can't help thinking about the nothingness of forever. "Call me weird," he said, "but it kind of freaks me out." I sympathize with the feeling. A shiver goes down my spine seeing a sky like this. Most people on Earth live in regions of substantial light pollution, and space is something only seen on TV. Witnessing an unfettered night sky for the first time doesn't always elicit delight; confusion is more like it. *What are we seeing? Has this been up there the whole time?* When confusion doesn't go away, it eventually becomes awe.

Having the entire visible universe up there can be daunting, but my astrophobic friend certainly wouldn't want it *not* to be there. We deserve a glimpse, and to decide for ourselves.

Seeing stars is a birthright, one of the major features of living on Earth, and the last islands of visibility are shrinking, their edges eaten away by human-made light. Satellite observations and recordings from the ground show a surge in illumination over the last few decades that has diminished the celestial view worldwide and is gradually making us night-blind.

Besides the useful Bortle scale, I measure sky quality by calling an urban view a *domesticated* sky. A *feral* sky would be past the suburbs, at least twenty miles outside city limits where urban stargazers take their telescopes. *Wild* has no human lights, no atmospheric glare from glowing filaments or diodes. You don't have to have a telescope, the entire sky becomes one. It's what I saw when I was a kid, my first eyeful of a full-dark night, which was not dark at all. This is old growth darkness where the trees of heaven grow all over each other, spangled in countless blossoms.

If I were a Johnny Appleseed of dark nights, I'd plant dazzling skies as I wander the land, tin pot for a hat, sleeping on the ground with no roof to block the view. The seeds are already in place, stars waiting to appear, nourished whenever the light fades out. I'd tend to these otherworldly forests by looking up and making eye contact. A night sky is not an absence of light, it is the presence of the universe. It is there to be seen. I'll take refuge beneath an overgrown, untamed cosmos where the ground shimmers even when there's no moon. I'll draw blankets of light-years over myself, in no hurry to fall asleep, eyes wide and sparkling with stars.

BORTLE 9

* * * * * * * * * * *

The entire sky is brightly lit, even at the zenith. Many stars making up familiar constellation figures are invisible, and dim constellations such as Cancer and Pisces are not seen at all. Aside from perhaps the Pleiades, no Messier objects are visible to the unaided eye. The only celestial objects that really provide pleasing telescopic views are the Moon, the planets, and a few of the brightest star clusters, which are difficult to find.

* * * * * * * * * * *

BORTLE 9

I wake underwater, holding my breath, not sure where I am or what time it is. The ceiling swims with ghostly blue fish that must have drifted in when I left the blinds open. Lifting my head from a cave of hotel room pillows, I'm surprised to find the air breathable. Floor-to-ceiling windows along one wall make the sky outside look strange, missing the stars that usually stitch the night together. The moon has loosened from its socket and fallen to the ground.

I sit up and a bucket of megawatts washes my face from the city outside. I reach for my phone on the nightstand and it's around four in the morning, just shy of dawn. The room feels like a psychedelic mansion. I pull my body and its sprawling appendages from under the covers and shamble over to the window, stepping through gear scattered all over the floor, a couple bikes stark black against the glass. Standing in my boxers, I put my hands on the window and look out from the twenty-seventh floor of a high-rise along the Las Vegas Strip. The world's largest globe-shaped building is at the bottom projecting the moon like a great hologram, a luminous mushroom pushing buildings aside.

Usually, this sphere—which is called, simply, *Sphere*—displays absurdly large ads for footwear or video games rolling around on the surface of the 300-foot-tall orb, but this early in the morning nobody is paying for advertising and few are awake to care. Some blessed soul working at an entertainment conglomerate decided to project a fully accurate moon rotating on its axis, turning from crescent to gibbous to full and back, like a blessing-hour given back to the city, payment for killing the night. This moon they've given us is so accurate I could be fooled into thinking it's real, except for it rolling around like a pig in a trough of hotels and parking structures.

I'm not waking well. Sleeping with the blinds open threw me off. Left on overnight, electric lights disrupt dream sleep and agitate the body's biological clock, known to create mental and physical disorders, something that could kill you or drive you mad if it happens too often. Being held indefinitely in a fully lit cell is considered a form of torture, a disassociation from reality and the passage of time. Based on the arrhythmic pulsing light I'm seeing out this window, we are inside of that bright box now. What has never occurred on Earth, not in its many-billion-year history of innumerable climate changes and extinction events, is happening now. There has never been this much light.

In the other bed my travel companion is asleep rolled up in bleached sheets, mildly jet-lagged from his flight from DC where he lives. He's an old friend, Irvin Fox-Fernandez, and in the decades we've known each other we've spent more than four hundred nights on the ground together, pupils of Earth and night sky. Our mission this time is simple and judicious: starting in the brightest part of Nevada—one of the most light-filled cities in the world—we'll trek with bicycles following a chain of supply caches to find the nearest full-dark sky. Our course is due north, straight out of Vegas. Two hardtail mountain bikes lean against the windows, and today, on the cusp of the new moon, we'll load them up like mules. I plan outings by the moon, keeping a chart of the year's phases taped to the fridge at home, and the new moon puts us under the darkest possible skies. Bikes aren't our forte, but they're the right conveyance for this journey, a human-powered pace through rugged terrain where we are neither speeding nor crawling. This should allow us to discern the change night by night as we go a couple hundred miles from the city. The human eye takes from fifteen minutes to an hour to adjust to unlit conditions, and I want to see what happens with ten concerted nights, a meditation on a deepening sky.

We saw ourselves off with a few drinks last night and I walked around with my handheld light meter pegging off the charts. Like a half-baked scientist, I held it up to fireworks and water shows on the Strip. Asked by passers-by what I was doing, I'd tell them I was recording ambient light from the sky and they'd smile, bemused, *oh, cool*. Sitting at a bar flashing with strobes, I held up my Sky Quality Meter, or SQM, and took numbers that jumped around with too many extremes for its sensitive optics to process.

In a chill early November wind, we wandered the city, Irvin in shorts and flip-flops, me in long pants and a light jacket. The blustering wind picked up to the point that we sought the sides of buildings and the shelter of giant, bright signs. Irvin's feet were cold. "It feels like I'm waking up!" he said.

It was time for a trip with Irvin, some years since we've had a good trek between us. He's a biologist and a lifer with the Forest Service, a right companion to enlighten a journey to the dark. We've been warned the roads we're using are excessively rough and in places they disappear into dry lake beds. We drove out ahead of time and left an array of water caches and food in buckets taped shut and buried or hidden in rock holes, each pinged with a GPS forming pins in a sea of dust, rock, and Joshua trees, our path into the night.

Before midnight, we walked to Sphere, cutting across streets and around formed concrete. Pulsing electric jellyfish rose three hundred feet over our heads, growing taller as we came near. This architectural behemoth has an exterior skin of LED pixels covering 580,000 square feet in all directions except for where it touches ground, the largest continuous projection screen in the world. With 256 million color variations emitted by 316 million individual LEDs, the object is a visual blastoma, and people living anywhere nearby say they can't stand how it paints their nightlives in luminous watercolors that leak between buildings and go on for blocks, perfectly visible from the city limits. Directly below its spherical belly, Irvin and I watched images overhead blending into a vibrant wash, which I imagine is the last thing a moth sees before it dies, hexagonal light receptors excited to an optical version of a scream.

Irvin, Filipino American with a beaming grin, came with a fresh crew cut, and I resemble a scruffy Santa Claus, both of us holding up our cameras alongside selfie-taking teenagers, loners in jackets, and families with kids spinning like tops. I pulled out my optic device, hardly bigger than a deck of cards, and lifted it overhead, pushing the button on its face. After a moment, it responded with a number in red LED. I pushed again and a completely different number appeared. A third time produced another, and none were related; 8.27, 14.70, 13.32. Meaningless. The device is meant for measuring ambient night skies, not these waves brighter in the blue-white spectrum than a full-bright day, worse for your eyes than the sun because you're compelled to stare at it. Which is what we did, Irvin coming in close to the towering orb with his body turning blue, red, and green. He stopped eye to eye with fleets of glowing electronic pucks. Each puck counts as a pixel mounted into a crisscrossing metal infrastructure that rose over our heads to take up most of the sky. He turned to me with his big, toothy smile and said, *what the hell is this?*

Being drawn to such a spectacle is a pure physical response, so the feeling we had of being on top of the world makes sense. It's called positive phototaxis, the natural movement of an organism toward light. Not all living things exhibit positive phototaxis, but most do. Lizards, fish, crabs, foxes, frogs do it. Plants lean in, moths are pros, and birds notoriously wheel toward any city, spinning over spotlights and streetlamps as if the maps in their almond-sized brains can't stop saying turn left, turn left, turn left. This gravitational pull toward light is aptly termed "trapping," and it often leads to the demise of creatures through simple exhaustion, or swift predation by opportunistic hunters drawn to the commotion, or crashing into windows.

Turn on a light, and a fly will enter the room.

Fleets of manta rays appear when coastal resorts shine spotlights into the ocean, luring plankton that draw the rays where tourists can swim in crowded, half-awkward underwater ballets.

In a forest in the Florida Panhandle, I flashed a headlamp beneath a canopy of loblolly pines and my field of vision quickly filled with hundreds of tiny green glints, the eyes of wolf spiders orienting themselves toward me.

My dad took me to the desert in southern Arizona on a moonless night and with a spotlight clipped onto a car battery he lured coyotes, streaks of fur and needle noses darting in close to see what's the matter.

On a single summer night in 2019, an estimated 48 million pallid-winged grasshoppers converged on Las Vegas from all directions—more than thirty tons of insects—bodies, wings, and legs saturating the airspace and covering sidewalks. The footage is alarming and mesmerizing: casino entrances besieged, the upcast skybeam of the Luxor turned into a writhing white static. They came because of the light, drawn just like us. This is one side of the coin, and on the other is a night sky so untrammeled that it is bright on its own and casts a shadow.

Positive phototaxis crosses all living genres, a code written into the earliest genes where even bacteria expand lightward instead of away. If you'd presented this projection sphere to early *Homo sapiens*, we would have gathered below it hooting and hollering, throwing rocks and sticks. We would not have turned our backs to it. Since then, we've learned to temper our flailing and shouting, which is why we remain relatively tranquil, taking pictures of ourselves with this sphere behind us, when what we really want is to flap our wings till they tatter.

—

Bortle is a naked-eye scale for determining a night sky's quality, first published in *Sky & Telescope* magazine in 2001 by amateur astronomer John E. Bortle. His name sounds space-like, as if, like Jan Oort of the Oort Cloud, it were destined for astronomical prominence. Known for documenting and publishing new comet sightings, Mr. Bortle devised a simple scale from 1 to 9 based on what you can and cannot see: Mars, or the globular fuzz patches of faraway Messier objects, or Zodiacal lights. Do the Sagittarius and Scorpio regions in the sky cast a shadow, or does artificial light cast a shadow?

Bortle 1, pinnacle of the scale, is a fourteen-carat night where only stellar light and backscatter from sunshine in space can be seen. Constellations are hard to make out, swallowed by so many stars they recede into a glistening fabric. Ripples in the larger atmosphere are sometimes visible, causing space to wave gently, and any passing cloud looks like a black hole.

The other end is Bortle 9, which has enough airborne light for easily reading from the page of a book. The atmosphere is gray, white, orange, or lemon, and clouds are wholly lit from below like steamships cruising across a bright ocean. That would be Las Vegas Boulevard along the Strip. If the scale allowed, I'd call this a 9+, as bright before 5 a.m. as 10 p.m. or midnight, moon or no moon.

Going from one end of the scale to the other by driving rather than biking would be far too swift, getting us to the deepest night in three or four hours. Walking a couple hundred miles would be too slow and I doubt we'd be able to perceive the incremental change. Bikes were the proper choice, and this was the proper starting place, moon fallen to the ground with almost all of the stars plucked out.

Before dawn, I come down the elevator with my bike, then descend an escalator with a tire on each step, letting off in a quiet lobby with lonely slot machines, and out the automatic glass door into Vegas. With wind on my cheeks almost cold enough to freeze, I click into a middle gear and aim toward the giant luminous orb several blocks away, hoping to catch it before the ads start up.

In the surrounding Mojave Desert, dawn cuts at mountain edges, but I am too deep into the city to see. Pedestrians have thinned to almost zero. Irvin's still asleep back in a room swimming with blue fish because I insisted on leaving the blinds open.

On the ground, security guards are on their phones, wearing parkas and layers of hoodies, bundled up for a cool desert dawn. I'm dressed in a windbreaker, shorts, and biking gloves. A flashing red LED hangs on my tail and I'm wearing a headlamp strapped to my helmet, more to help cars see me. Bike tires buzz and bump over power cables and iron planks placed across holes in the streets, construction going up everywhere, the morning cranes as still as mantises.

A big race, the Formula 1 Grand Prix, is about to materialize, putting a seven-mile asphalt loop in the middle of the already hopped-up center of everything, an architectural jungle gym, a rat maze for a person on a bicycle where concrete barriers and flashing signs shine in every direction. Workers trying to get to their jobs complain about the extra hour their commute takes through colosseum seating, metal beams, and aluminum tracks. An echelon of stadium lights has gone in and they are all on, the city burning itself, brightness on the shoulders of brightness. I don't think it's the cold that makes my skin feel like it's vibrating. There's something else—the electromagnetic fields I'm passing through, or maybe the simple fact that I live near a town in Colorado with a population of five hundred, a place several thousand times less lit up than Vegas. At this time of morning, you'd see only headlights from a single ranch truck on the highway as the town nearby lies quiet under its stars.

Vegas makes me nervous and excited, what I believe is called anxiety, what most people must feel as a constant background in this city, so much happening we can't look away and we can't get away. I catch glimpses of the fabricated moon where its shines between posts and beams. Security details in hard hats sit on boxes and folding chairs. They think about redirecting me as I weave through Grand Prix infrastructure with its wheelbarrows, forklifts, and flats of bottled water stacked into crystalline cubes. Without slowing, I receive a bored nod to say *go ahead*; too cold for them to get up and wave me to stop.

A gap between piers opens onto a concrete floor egg-washed in digital light. A three-hundred-foot-tall simulacrum of the moon rotates overhead with an inaudible groan. I stop, lean on one leg, and pull out my phone to take pictures. I can't say I hate it. The truth is, I love it. Doused in its greatness, I feel like I'm part of a rising wave of civilization that feels like it's bringing everyone up with it like a flood, depending on what you call *up*. If the measurement is light, most of us are in it. Per unit area, this is the most amply lit city in North America, and the recently opened Sphere bumps the number. People who want our civilization to be king of the hill say this is not the work of a late-stage empire, but a city in its prime, nowhere to go but up. I'd consider in this argument the pyramid-temples that rose at the end of the Mayan Empire, or King Nebuchadnezzar II's Ishtar Gate just before the fall of Babylon. We do great things until the very end. The pattern is familiar.

I need to shake off this monumental sense of wonder and get perspective. Late stage, middle, or early isn't ours to decide. Past the spherical monstrosity's curve floats the actual moon in space, a waning crescent in the east, and the pinhole brightness of Venus next to it. Whatever sense of wonder this luminous and literal eyesore produces, the real moon in space dwarfs it, even a cat-scratch crescent. I dismount and walk the bike across a concrete surface, and I'm a little sci-fi man looking up into a lit sky, my body painted and swirled, the concrete beneath me reflecting the same. A security guard on the other side of a wire fence pauses to watch me take pictures. He follows my view, fixing on the crescent moon. He's older than the guards at the gates, middle-aged and jolly of stature, same as me, beard a little trimmer and showing some gray. In an Amharic accent, he asks, "Are you a tourist?"

I say yes and he says he usually doesn't see tourists out this early.

He gestures with his chin at the sky, asking what I see, and I point to the crescent. As I wheel my bike over to him, I tell him that's Venus next to it.

He wears a warm cap and a yellow vest with a lanyard around his neck. "So that's Venus?" he asks.

"It's only visible when it's closer to the horizon," I say. "Dawn or dusk, like this."

He seems pleased to know it's a planet, saying he wasn't sure if he was watching an airplane or a helicopter because it didn't appear to move. I point to the west and tell him Jupiter is over there, which appears blue and then green. We both look up and after a moment of quiet he says, "Where I grew up in Ethiopia, we had incredible stars. You could look up and see God."

He has a kind face taken with thought, and later in the conversation I'd learn about his daughter going to school here, him moving his family from Hawai'i, and how he doesn't see real night anymore, wondering if we're not in a computer simulation at this point. He says, "I wonder what it does to us not to see the night sky?"

At first, I think what are the chances of meeting such a person at the start of a nocturnal journey? Then I think that when you're aligning with the cosmos, the chances of whatever's happening are always 100 percent. I say this is exactly what I'm working on, trying to get to the darkest of the dark from here, using this bike to get there, and he doesn't seem surprised, taking it with a studious *hmm*. I pull out a recorder and ask about the skies of his youth. "Oh, they were beautiful," he says as his voice gathers strength. "I mean, in my imagination I could see the whole of space full of stars."

His eyes are beaming as he talks, and I don't know what kind of horizon he's remembering from Ethiopia, but I can see that sky in my mind, stars so numerous and crisp it feels as if they're parting like water around your shoulders.

"Maybe it's because all this light," he says. "Because I've driven out of Vegas where there's no light, and it's not like the stars I used to see. They used to feel so close when I was a child. Maybe my eyesight is not as good as it used to be."

Maybe he needs to get farther from Vegas, but I agree, eyesight can be a problem, and as we talk, I learn we're both in our mid-fifties, hardly a year apart. He gestures with his chin at the civilization on display around us and says, "This all seems very tenuous, right?"

"It does," I say, not just to go along with him but because I believe it, feeling as if we've been balancing one card atop the last for centuries, if not thousands of years. Who doesn't feel the fragility hidden within this show of strength we put on?

He says, "To be honest, nothing positive has come from Western civilization. You know, extinctions of wildlife and plants, and our seas turning acidic, overfished, and polluted. In two hundred years, we've become a cancer to this planet. We've metastasized."

I agree with him again, but not entirely. There are more than just our horrors. But what can you say? Fight the good fight. It's a lot to share between two strangers bathed in world-changing incandescence, one that astronauts see as they pass in orbit, like cosmic oncologists pointing out the singular growth of Las Vegas in a black sweep of desert. In the first morning blue, the guard and I reach through the fence to grip hands, thanking each other for the encounter. Dawn unfolds into sunrise as I bike back toward our lodgings, the guard's question settling inside of me, what does it do to us not being able to see the night sky?

In 1729, French scientist Jean-Jacques d'Ortus de Mairan placed a plant in a light-proof room to see what having no day or night would do to it. He chose a mimosa, which opens its leaves in the morning and closes them in the evening. De Mairan was an astronomer who cataloged features of the night sky, having a nebula and an impact crater on the moon named after him. He was also the owner of a vineyard in southern France where he studied botany, thus his interest in sky events influencing plants. He found that the frills of the mimosa's leaves continued their pattern of opening and closing on a twenty-four-hour schedule whether or not they received input from outside, and he theorized that something other than the sun must trigger this daily routine, something inside the plant itself aligned with the turning of the planet. This is how De Mairan famously stumbled onto the concept of circadian rhythm.

The day and night cycle is fundamental to about every living thing, dating back to the first organisms on Earth. As the theory goes, when the sun burned through a thin, almost nonexistent atmosphere some three and a half billion years ago, fragile strands of DNA sizzled under the light. The only escape was at nighttime when these nascent cells could avoid the beating of radiation, when they could divide and mend themselves. They needed light for energy, reaching toward it, and in the dark they made quiet repairs. Genetic oscillators became an evolutionary step, the ability to anticipate severe environmental change occurring in twenty-four-hour cycles, flipping to a different chemical and metabolic regime for day and night.

Circa diem means "about a day." In humans, circadian rhythm drives feeding, rest, activity, body temperature, digestion, hormone release, cellular repair—basically our entire biological infrastructure. While plants for the most part have twenty-four hours hardwired into them, humans, most mammals, and many vertebrates and invertebrates are more finely tuned, fitted with optic nerves that react directly to light. We're a diurnal species, less active at night and bustling during the day. This should sound familiar, the swooning, restorative perfumes of evening, and hard work when the sun comes up. We have chemistry for each.

The center of the biological clock in humans is a densely packed nut of neurons called the suprachiasmatic nucleus, seated at the back of the hypothalamus and connected directly to our retinas. While the eyes allow the brain to see light, the suprachiasmatic nucleus is how the rest of the body interprets it. As we sleep, a dim light through the eyelids is enough to unsettle the day-night pattern, causing hormonal imbalances because the nucleus hasn't been allowed to fully switch to from light mode to dark. With six hours or more of bright light at night, darkness fails to reset the system, and the body's timer goes back to zero. The suprachiasmatic nucleus is only the top of the chain, and below it every cell in the body has its own circadian governor. Every part of us is a clock set to a spinning Earth, perhaps the most reliable element we've ever had.

Light itself isn't the problem; it's the lack of dark. Both are needed. Rats exposed to dim, continuous light at night have impaired glucose processing, increased fat deposits, elevated body mass, and generally broken metabolic chemistry. When they're returned to a natural balance of half light and half dark, the problems subside.

When light doesn't go off, the problems worsen. A study from 1964 found that mice exposed to constant light grew mammary tumors. The same was later found in humans. By the mid-1980s, the connection between excess artificial light and breast cancer was a fact. In 2017, researchers overlaid two maps of 147 communities in Israel, one a map of light concentrations, the other showing clusters of breast cancer. Not surprisingly, the two matched. Women in well-lit areas had a 63 percent increase in risk compared to women in less-lit areas. Of course, artificial light comes with a host of other factors: sedentary lifestyles, processed foods, and the presence of concentrated, toxic chemicals. The problem is many faceted, and it comes with the company of artificial light letting us stay up later doing more of whatever we were doing all day. Nightshift workers seem to have it worst, experiencing an increased risk of obesity, heart disease, high blood pressure, high cholesterol, diabetes, stroke, mood disorders, depression, suicide, and a host of cancers. This labor force didn't exist before electricity's glowing filaments turned nighttime into an extension of daytime, opening a gateway to disease and hormonal disruption. Medical institutions have labeled this kind of work carcinogenic, and in 2009, Norway began paying reparations to female shift workers who developed breast cancer.

Starting in the 1980s, Dr. Richard Stevens, a cancer epidemiologist at the University of Connecticut, pioneered the study of light and breast cancer, finding the circadian rhythm to be its linchpin. Melatonin, a hormone that naturally rises at night and falls during the day, is inversely associated with estrogen, which alters cellular activity in breast tissues. Melatonin and estrogen are biochronological, timed in sequence. If the pattern is off, estrogens and melatonin trip over each other, too much of one, not enough of the other, and they do so in no particular order.

Asked what could be done to reverse the trend, Stevens answered that simply turning down the lights in the evening would help. "Get it dimmer," he said.

To answer the guard's question of what it does to us not to see the night sky, it is inexorably killing us.

Sunlight arrives in hundred-foot-tall slices, one landing brightly on a Ferris wheel that looks like it belongs on Jupiter. Too early to sell tickets, it hasn't started turning.

The highest buildings are touched first. Amber banners of sunlight loosen down their faces where I keep to the shadows below, pedaling through half-filled parking lots, under barriers, and along side streets. Shift workers disperse out of the backs of casinos, released toward parking lots and alleys to find their cars and catch buses into the day, which is their version of nighttime. As I bike around them, I wonder if they know the dangers of their jobs, thinking they deserve hazard pay for how little dark they experience.

When the sun reaches me, it will feel good on my fingers, chilly from a cool, breezy morning. The sun coming up in this city is a relief, and it is far easier on the eyes than the macular degeneration of LEDs. The cold light of diodes damages structures inside the eye, causing retinal cells to weaken and tear. This is what our genius is doing to us.

People emerging in dealer's vests and kitchen shirts after their shifts must appreciate the sheer fact of the sun, how it shifts between buildings, palm trees, and parking structures. If not consciously, they are bodily aware of their clocks seeking a hold, asking, is this it? Is this the light of actual sunrise?

I'm sorry, people. We should at least give you a planetarium for your breaks.

When I reach the Strip, I stay on the shady side of the boulevard, easing into the day. Later, we will depart from Vegas, no more tiki bars after this. When we reach whatever night sky we're looking for at the other end—midnight blues and sheens of cosmic dust floating between planets—we should bottle some of that sky and bring it back where we'd stand behind casinos handing out vials like aid workers.

I get off my bike and walk it past open mouths of clown-like buildings with revelers winnowed down to those who had a great run last night and the majority who did not. Raucous shouts come out of glass doors sliding open, and a gang of friends convulses down the sidewalk, their wings tattered, antennae burned to nubs.

My day is only starting, and I'm in a different mood, jaunty as I walk, steering my handlebars through morning joggers who pass in ones and twos, women with dogs, men running in place at an intersection waiting for the light to change. We are the first pedestrians of the day shift, saying hello to each other, exchanging quips about how this fine turquoise sky is shaping up, the privilege of a night's rest. Left past Planet Hollywood, I walk my bike around a corner into the sun where I'm branded by a blast of nuclear fusion. If my oscillators weren't flipped, they are now.

BORTLE 8

* * * * * * * * * * *

The sky glows whitish gray or orangish, and you can read newspaper headlines without difficulty. M31 and M44 may be barely glimpsed by an experienced observer on good nights, and only the bright Messier objects are detectable with a modest-size telescope. Some of the stars making up the familiar constellation patterns are difficult to see or are absent entirely.

* * * * * * * * * * *

BORTLE 8

Three hours till sunset, the need to exit Las Vegas is urgent. Our eyes are focused on what's immediately ahead of us, our bikes loaded heavy, pedals pumping as we ferry gear through a cold-blooded tangle of traffic. We'd been watching the streets, waiting for a cessation, any kind of slowing, but none came. Rush hour is every hour. We haven't been out yet fully loaded like this, our trail bikes low-geared with fat, toothy tires buzzing on asphalt. Irvin is a little sloppy on his balance out ahead of me because he hasn't dealt with this weight distribution before, dodging under the mirror of a parked construction truck and, a second and a half later, a mirror craned out from a transport bus. He has panniers on the rear, his tail heaped with compression sacks strapped tight, handlebars rigged with whatever they can hold, water bottles attached to the forks of the front wheel. My bike is loaded much like his, and I'm ten feet behind him swerving through afternoon light, teetering just as much as I perform the same pitches and yaws, head ducking around the same out-reaching mirrors. It's impossible not to be sloppy less than a minute out of the gates and into this kind of congestion.

With the Formula 1 race in town, the mood on the street is vile. Drivers seem murderous. Everywhere we go is a detour. No one is supposed to be here, certainly not us. We only get through because we're moving faster than everyone else in a bottleneck ground halfway to a halt, anyone in motion in the act of cutting someone else off. LED arrow boards flash for everyone to merge from both sides into an apocalyptic gridlock, sirens wailing in the distance, drivers mashing the heels of their palms into horns. *The zombies have escaped. Leave the city immediately.*

A man in neon construction garb throws up hand signals, either telling us to get the hell off the street or stopping the hungry, growling work truck behind us from bearing down on my ass. A bus puts on its blinker and pushes Irvin toward the corner of a flatbed loaded with metal barricades. He makes it through, and I squeeze behind him by inches, Irvin flicking his head to see if I made it. We pass plastic barrel barricades and signs: NO LEFTS, NO RIGHTS, ONE WAY, DETOUR, ROAD CLOSED AHEAD. If I weren't paying so much attention to what's right in front of me, I might start screaming. I don't mind being on foot on a sidewalk where I can move around like a primate, but on a bike, I'm riding bareback in a steeplechase, the horse's mane gripped in my fists, my fate out of my control—and I don't even like riding horses.

Irvin wears a buttoned-down field shirt, cuffs pulled to his wrists, and green baggy shorts with no racing stripes or sponsor logos. Between us, we can fix a flat if needed, true a tire, crack and suture a chain. Tool kit, pump, water, whatever we pared down to at the hotel we have with us. Irvin was a Boy Scout growing up in bright and sunny Southern California, the son of an immigrant family, and by fifteen, he was an Eagle Scout. We met in our twenties working for an outdoor education outfit leading city kids in the wilderness, and shortly after that, he was off to West Africa studying hornbills and forest ecology for grad school. Then, he worked as a wildlife biologist for the National Wildlife Refuge System in San Diego and moved from there to the US Forest Service as a field biologist and resource officer, and occasional firefighter. He's had a kid. I've had two. My once-black beard has turned white, and his hair doesn't have a touch of silver at the age of fifty-three.

He bikes for pleasure around DC, and I assume he's more comfortable dodging metal than I am, but when we reach a stoplight, and I get a flash of his eyes, he's got as much white in them as I do.

We both fear for our lives. I'm not looking for options. There's no way out but to go straight as long as we can. We're at an unholy intersection of seven lanes meeting at once, overrun by scaffolding and red cones. Irvin holds himself and his bike with one hand on a concrete barrier and with the other, he taps the screen on his phone, which is strapped to the console of his handlebars. Looking up and then back to the screen, he sees that the streets are not where they are supposed to be and everything is upended. We don't say anything out loud because no one wants to say *whose shitty idea was this?* The plan made sense when we first talked about it, taking off from our hotel and heading for the outskirts, escaping ground zero with enough velocity to pitch us into space.

Green light, go; skim by concrete barriers; get to the right but not all the way right because it's got rock cobbles, chunks of tire rubber, and sharp metal pieces. The big, car-washed trucks are the worst, the bullies of the street, their bald metal foreheads forcing us out of the way. The city sizzles with energy; again, the vibration in my skin, all chemistry in my body turned up, senses set to high. A primal urge for exigency is being satisfied, dull everyday trauma answered with traffic. Is there any place in the average person's experience where there's this much likelihood of sudden catastrophe? Everyone feels it, the heads behind windshields, steering wheels gripped. If push came to shove, Irvin and I would lose.

I'm on his tail like a shadow, tucked behind his back tire. It's four in the afternoon, and daylight begins to relax in the west. Crossing West Flamingo Road with its gaudy off-strip casinos and blocks of parking structures, I can see a crumple of tawny-colored mountains twenty miles off, a place of arroyos and coyotes, and out past the burnt-out couches and bullet-riddled washing machines where there will be nothing but rock and the bristled gorgons of Joshua trees. That's where we need to be, still hours away.

Like other cities in the West, Las Vegas looks as if it was dropped like a bomb. Founded in 1905, it was initially a lone stop along railroad tracks stretched across the Mojave Desert, a crushed-rock landscape of mountain ranges laid like reptile spines around vast, dry basins. The atmosphere at the turn of the century would have been mostly silent, touched by far-off winds. The first dirt streets came together around a wooden First State Bank, and within a year of founding, an electric power company was established, bringing streetlights and nighttime signage, a prickle in the darkness.

Eighty years before that, a Spanish trade caravan came through on its way to Los Angeles, and entering this broad and riverless basin, the party watered at a cluster of spring water streams converging on a natural field of dark-tipped rushes and luxuriant grass. The traders called this place Las Vegas, the meadows. They camped with hobbled horses, the ground pressed hard by barefoot and sandaled Indios living around here, mostly Southern Paiute people, the Nuwu. There were no buildings, no electric lights back then, no kerosene, and no boardwalks. A simple wood fire is all they would have had. Looking up from its flicker, the Spanish traders would have seen the same quality of sky that the Nuwu had known for centuries, the same sky seen by Uto-Aztecan-speaking ancestors a thousand years earlier, people who ate grass seeds and rabbit, and fish from a river a two-day walk to the east. Before them came Desert Archaic cultures, makers of stone tools dating back four thousand years or more, who saw the same sky, as did the people of the Pleistocene who lived among mammoths and ground sloths. At a certain point, dark is dark, which it is no longer.

Looking down from space a couple thousand years ago, flickers of empire would have been visible across the world, early ventures into massive public lighting. Mayan city-states would have stood out in what is now Central America, lit by causeways of fire around great temple complexes like Chichén-Itzá, Tikal, Palenque. At night, on auspicious dates and at royal coronations, innumerable fires were set along broad avenues and up the stairs of pyramids. From orbit, you would have known something was happening, an early notch in the belt of artificial illumination. This could be called the start of the age of light.

Despite this, Central American skies were as dark as ever. Civilization growing there paid meticulous attention to celestial mechanics, accurately predicting eclipses, assembling calendars based not only on Earth time but on the periodicity of planets, which restarts every forty-five years, longer and far more detailed than what Gregorians much later thought up. Wars were waged depending on the positions of planets as ceremonial fires at the start of the year were lit in the biggest temples before being carried to lesser temples, then to great houses, and then homes and villages. Runners brought fire to far communities, lighting altars and hearths, and thus began a tenuous worldwide balance that we struggle with today, artificial light rising as we try to hold onto our skies.

Simultaneously on the other side of the planet, the brightest human-made light of its day was constructed in the city of Alexandria on the coast of Egypt, another area lighting up in the last thousand years BC. Written records and archaeological finds tell of stone and metal cauldrons holding temple fires that would have warmed the faces of statues and frescos. Granite columns flickered with long, perfect shadows. Ancient Greece was only a variation on what was happening with the Mayan Empire; the scale and precision of architecture and population levels were similar, both cultures erecting temples to sky gods in their own ways. At the head of the city, aiming out to sea, stood this largest of all lighting devices, the Pharos of Alexandria, a monument of stone architecture rising more than three hundred feet tall, its summit holding a bonfire visible to mariners thirty miles away. During the day, its smoke could have been spotted 140 miles offshore. Long after this lighthouse fell into ruins, toppled by earthquakes and disrepair, it was acclaimed as one of the Seven Wonders of the World, one of history's more remarkable feats.

Originally, the Pharos of Alexandria had the luster of pearl, its exterior faced in blocks of white travertine, the kind of thing J. R. R. Tolkien might have dreamed up, an ivory tower with a fiery eye at its peak. Causeways ascending the interior were wide enough for oxen that may have hauled firewood carts, hooves nicking rock as loads of brush, bramble, and papyrus roots rattled upward flight after flight. Wood was fed continuously into a broad cresset before a polished-metal mirror. Golden bodies shimmered, dressed down to skin, hurling in wood and arranging it with poles. Legend had it that this pinnacle of light could be directed at ships in the harbor to set them ablaze. If you saw the Pharos for the first time, you would have thought that this was possible. It must have struck fear in the hearts of adversaries plotting to attack the city by sea at night, where the light of the gods had been brought down to Earth.

One of the half a million people living in Alexandria at the time was mathematician and astronomer Claudius Ptolemy. From his perch in the city, Ptolemy could see such a clear sky he was able to make tables showing how to predict eclipses, as well as the orderly setting and rising of the sun, moon, planets, and prominent stars. Building on the astronomical works of the Babylonians before him, Ptolemy made what might be called an early astronomy app, an outline of conjunctions and occultations, an almanac for the visible universe. I imagine he'd be confounded if he could see how we breeze through his quandaries today, how we don't have to understand a lick about the function of the heavens, finding answers in nanoseconds off our phones by glancing down instead of up. He also would be startled to realize how little of the sky can be seen today. He'd think we are deliberately blinding ourselves.

At the time, Greeks and their kin generally believed that stars were near to us, moving through a glimmering ether not far above the clouds. Trained in precise measurements and relationships between celestial bodies, Ptolemy thought otherwise. The stars, he believed, were very far away, their distances hard to fathom. He thought they were about twenty thousand times the radius of the

Earth away from us. That was immensely off from actual distances measured in light-years, but two thousand years ago, this was as far as the mind could go.

Our bearded first-century scientist must have strolled the temples late at night as open air drifted through polished stone ambulatories. Looking up from one of the largest cities in the world, he would have seen a frosting of stars and recognized many of them, knowing constellations by names still used today. Most people of that era would have done the same, half of their breathing hours spent under the infinite ceiling of outer space.

With the light of the Pharos nearby, Ptolemy was probably in a Bortle 2 sky, one short step from the darkest possible night. A thousand abacuses would have turned overhead as he rattled through tables and questions. Every science of his day was founded on the meticulous study of the cosmos, where planets were referred to as Astra Planeta; *astra* meaning "star" and *planeta* meaning "wanderer" or "wandering stars." With his hand resting against a fluted column, Ptolemy could look at his subject eye to eye. Half a million people around him with their lamps and hearth fires, even the Pharos at full power, could not have dimmed what he saw.

I like to imagine him coming home from a rousing night of wine and discourse by clay oil lamp, pausing for a few moments, slightly liquored up under the countless stars of Alexandria. Above him, he would have seen a skyful of gods, and the astronomer's lips would have parted in awe as if he'd lost the ability to speak.

Here in Nevada, the gray clouds of mountains in the distance have drawn closer, one wrapping its arm around another, ridge over ridge. The sun will drop behind them in half an hour. We've found a mercifully wide bike lane hugging lighter suburban traffic where we push up the long, gradual incline of the Las Vegas Basin.

By dark, we need to be out of the danger of moving vehicles

and onto a secured bike path that will get us to the city limits. Irvin has the lead as a lens-flare sunset starts ahead of us. We're hopping sidewalks, crosscutting streets, and passing through a swatch of land that has yet to be developed, a scrap of desert left between a ballpark and a palm-treed neighborhood. Getting across it is messy. Tires spin for grip in sandy cobble, hillocks of creosote bushes around us like witches' brooms. Based on the pace of growth in Vegas, I'd give this island of windblown grocery bags and half-buried plastic cups five years before it's been paved and completely illuminated.

A few minutes before sunset, my front tire flies sideways in a dustbin of rocks, spinning out from under me, and the bike and I pitch over. A grunt knocks out of me as my face lands in a fist of burro weed. I groan and pull myself out from under the bike, lifting the weight of me and my loaded machine into golden light. I think Ptolemy would have approved. However clumsy we might appear—however clumsy I actually seem to be—Irvin and I are on an expedition for the sky. Ptolemy would have lamented the burning of the Library of Alexandria, the loss of so much learning, and so much that has changed since then. Still, circumstances being as they are, I believe we'd at least get a nod for effort, for having our gear packed with star charts and recording equipment.

In the sulfuric light of dusk, we cross over a roaring interstate and reach a concrete bike path on the other side. Stopping to adjust gear, tighten up, and pull out jackets, we're relieved to be off the streets and random dirt lots, with several miles left to get us out of the fray. Headlights and streetlamps have come on. White towers pierce the pinkness of the sky, each carrying fourteen high-tension powerlines crackling above us. It feels like a land of mechanical giants fed by a constant blood flow of vehicles with headlights like rhinestones poured into a funnel. Atop the buttress of the overpass where we've stopped, an enlarged replica of ancient petroglyphs has been stamped into terracotta-colored concrete, a line of bighorn sheep posed as if dancing. This is public art, a Nuwu ancestral memory from the region, Southern Paiute heritage, cast over eight lanes of Interstate 215 as if to say *Look up and see where you are!*

In the 1990s, Irvin and I worked for an outdoor company taking teenage schoolkids from Los Angeles into the desert of the Lower Colorado River on the Arizona-California border. It was a ragged country of rock, cactus, and a night sky unaffected by us, about 150 miles to San Diego on one side, and Phoenix the same distance on the other. Our sites were suspended in the middle.

Some of the kids we took out had never seen real stars and had little idea they actually existed. You can imagine how they looked up, and some muttered things like, "Those are there all the time?" By night two, satellites were an accepted fact. You'd tell them find a satellite and within seconds someone would point one out. On clear nights, of which there were many, the stars came in such profusion that constellations were challenging to distinguish, needles in haystacks, more stars than empty space. We gave astronomy talks, and I don't know if anyone was listening. Instead, they looked up as if something dangerous were overhead. We had canoes on this flat, tepid stretch of river, and I'd take them into reedy backwaters at night and have the kids raft their canoes side by side and stow their paddles. The inlet fell silent after coots quieted in the reeds and kids stopped banging and rearranging. We lay on our backs against cushions of life jackets and stared straight up. Maybe I'd tell a story, some words to add context, but mostly it was quiet. I wanted them to decide for themselves what they were seeing. What questions do we not have when we aren't aware of the stars? What pieces of evolution are missing from our matrix?

The Milky Way cast a thin shadow, and I had the kids lift their hands to see how they'd become blackness, while the sky seemed like a flame of itself, a color of celestial light. I told them they were seeing *space light*, most of it coming from among planets and stars.

I could have gone on about how space isn't empty, how it has kind of a texture, and the particles floating in it, even if they are thousands of miles apart, add up to a sheen you can see from Earth. I held back and listened with the rest of them to the sky. A meteorite zipped overhead, swift white streak, an object the size of a baseball vaporized in half a second as it struck the atmosphere. Its trail remained visible for one second and no longer. The phosphorescent ghost faded as soon as we saw it, those few who happened to be looking in that quadrant. In the stillness among the canoes, I heard one girl quietly say, "What was that?"

When my two kids were young, we followed the moon together on a backpack trip through an eroded shale desert in western Colorado. I pulled them out of school and had to give an education-related excuse for their absence, so I said I was teaching them how to calculate when and where the moon will rise from one day to the next. It was an astro-geography lesson. They took notes so they could remember how it was done to report back to their teachers. If you want to learn celestial bodies, the moon is a starting place, our nearest sizable relation. Everyone sees it, no matter how washed-out the sky. We started the walk on a waxing gibbous, and we noted that it rose fifty minutes later each day, putting it closer and closer to sunset. We held up compasses, marked bearings, and each day added fifty minutes, and the moon appeared right on time, exactly where we said it would, burning its way out of a ridge-lined horizon in the east. Fourteen and eleven years old, my kids were serious about this endeavor and giddy each time it worked, a tiny spark firing in their heads answering the human need for discovery. Our last night, we set camp in naked hills and the full moon rose as the sun set, as if the two had an agreement. This symmetry is something you can rely on, I told them. The full moon will always appear just as the sun disappears. Let this be one of the givens.

I built a small fire that night, burning whatever we found, brittle pieces of dead and wind-rotted shadscale, years-old cow dung, and bits of coal we'd collected from a seam in a canyon two days earlier. The old cow dung smelled like dry, burning grass, and the coal was like the inside of an oil barrel. The wood smelled sour as it burned. I kept the fire going that night as the moon rose higher, it's creamy light falling through clouds. The kids chased each other across hillsides, shouting, laughing, as waves of lunar light landed on, then hid them.

The next day, we walked out of the desert, dusty and wild-haired, into the airport in Grand Junction, Colorado, where we boarded a direct flight to Las Vegas. I wanted to tack on an urban experience to our nature trek, so they'd know that a kind of wild exists in both places, you just have to have the eye to find it. They grew up in the lower Bortles with their mom and me, off-grid with a wood stove for heat, and it was agreed they needed healthy doses of civilization. Our plan was for the three of us to continue backpacking through Vegas the way we had in ridges and hills, staying in different hotels along the Strip and each night being in position for the moonrises. We found buildings to stand between and a monorail platform high enough to see an eastern horizon, compasses pulled out and pointed until the squashed egg of a post-full-moon came up right where we said it would.

On our last night in Vegas, we took an elevator to the top of the Stratosphere, a bell-bottomed pillar of concrete and steel that stands more than a thousand feet tall like an exclamation point at the end of the Strip. An open-air observation deck encircles the capsule on top where we swept binoculars across the bright gridlock below. A cool breeze whipped up as we watched an orange and waning gibbous moon rise behind ragged ranges beyond the Colorado River. The older kid began explaining to the younger how lunar gravitational forces cause tides, with one fist clenched in the air to represent the moon, the other to show the Earth. I didn't have to say a thing, as if this were the most natural way for children to talk, as if they were Greeks or Mayans in waiting.

That night I counted about twenty stars from the viewing platform. Getting above street level helped. We'd risen from Bortle 9 to 8, wiping a small hole from the sky where we could peek through to the other side.

The pearlescent dome of the city takes in every horizon, and flushes into space. On the Strip, Irvin and I had been in the limelight, attention brought to a point, with everything else burned out, three or four stars all I could get. Limelight is an intense non-electric fixture used a century and a half ago at the front of stages to show performers. The word is derived from burning calcium oxide, known as quicklime, which is the brilliance of the sky from the middle of Vegas.

Several miles into the suburbs, tonight's sky is more like lime itself, the citrus, not the stage lighting. It has the luminosity of a bin of limes under grocery store glare.

Irvin has a red beam mounted on his handlebars, and I've got a green one strapped to my helmet. We use these not so much to see as to make sure anyone coming our way sees us as we follow a paved bike trail around the city's perimeter. The trip is planned without white lights. We're sticking to the wavelengths of green and red which preserve night vision. At this point, the idea of night vision is a joke. I-215 passes along our right shoulders, southbound headlights like fire strikers sparking against our eyes. I calculate a few hundred cars a minute, five sets of headlights per second out of the corner of my eye.

Irvin signals a break and pulls in at sitting benches overlooking a grassy ballpark. Like something out of a modern druidic ritual, the mown field is encircled by LED torches up on poles, while the grounds are obviously sacred and unused, no one there, grass is lit up as brightly as garnish in a sushi case. Autumn air feels like the Mojave Desert, low fifties and dropping. Irvin pulls out a coat, telling me he's exhausted and dizzy. Getting through the city burned up most of our enthusiasm. "It's all that meat," I say, referring to earlier today, sausages and slices of smoked beef in an all-you-can-eat restaurant attached to a hive of casinos. Loading up on protein requires much water to digest, and insufficient water leads to dehydration, muscle cramping, dizziness. That's my guess.

"Or it's all these headlights," he says.

That, too.

Now that he mentions it, I'm feeling a bit dizzy. I hold up the SQM, and after four readings, I come up with an average magnitude of twelve, brighter than the inside of the bar last night. The device still isn't working right, not meant for taking readings in cities.

The ballpark looks like a plug of flesh extracted from the night. Most of the illumination being generated backscatters in all directions, a waste of energy and usefulness unless the point is to drown any remaining darkness. Excess light, by definition, means much of it goes where it's neither wanted nor needed. Fixtures around the ballpark have been fitted with shields so they don't shine straight up, but it goes up anyway, bouncing off the lens of mown grass, making a nearby high-tension power pylon gleam like marble.

A man walks across the field, throwing a frisbee to his dog. When the frisbee is airborne, it looks like a comet. Their crossing takes about a minute before they move off and the space is again empty, now lonelier.

The rest of the night we bike along a milky mountain range with subdivisions lifted along its flanks a few hundred feet above the bottom of the basin. The Strip pulses and fumes ten miles away and the city from up here resembles a well-lit aquarium, its water set to glowing. You can see everything. We pass homes with dining room windows showing off its people inside, a family sitting at a table, a couple working in a kitchen. Subdivisions become barren, unbuilt, populated only by cobra-head streetlights standing where neighborhoods are yet to be constructed. Thousands of ghostly lots pass by, future porch lights, future lives. For protection, lights are left on, deterring trespassers, although if we went biking in there we could set up camp on one of the lots and no one would notice.

It's ten at night and we're walking bikes uphill toward soft mirrors of mountains. Subdivisions dissolve into the last waving flags of grand openings. Past port-a-potties at construction sites, we roll by metal water towers, crunching across desert limestone, headlamps used so we don't walk the bikes over broken glass or discarded screws or nails. Our red and green lamps find a turntable crashed like a spaceship, and the drum of a washing machine caved in and shot up, as if we were a submersible cruising the sea floor. Trees of yucca with bayonets for leaves grow out here, and a few scraggly Joshua trees with bladed fists, poised as if ready to hold back the city. These are *Yucca brevifolia*, arms holding heads dressed in crowns, a bristled tree form of the yucca plant. They define this desert the way saguaros define the Sonoran, the way redwoods hug the edge of northern California. Camp is nowhere in particular, wherever we decide to stop. We're tired enough not to cook, sprawled in our nest of gear, bikes dropped on their sides in half-light.

We don't know who is out here. For a species that relies on visual acuity, being unable to see can be distressing. I wouldn't be surprised to see headlights suddenly coming upon us, and it would not make me comfortable. If there were a dangerous part of our trip, it's probably tonight, though I grew up in a big desert city with marching subdivisions, and I made this kind of quarter-dark a place of refuge where I liked to go at night and shrug off at least some of the city.

If Irvin and I were women, we'd be subject to more pressing concerns, the fear of violation and violence closer. It's a dubious privilege not having to pay much attention. Study after study has found that women and men walk differently in cities at night, female eyes tending to focus on areas outside a walking path, such as bushes and dark areas, while the male focus tends to be on the path ahead. In college, I was close with a woman who wanted the experience of walking on a city street alone at night and going wherever she wanted, so she asked a few of us to stay within view, far enough away she wasn't aware of us, lurking body guards. It was an experiment, or, more, an opportunity. She was six feet tall, a big-shouldered gal from a Colorado ranch town, and this was her wish, to walk in a city at night and not feel afraid. As we followed at a polite distance, she tended toward the lesser traveled sidewalks under trees that offered shade from streetlights. She moved candidly, pausing at will. Afterward she seemed exhilarated, like she'd gotten to see something hidden all her life.

Illuminating urban spaces makes detecting potential threats easier, but it is also blinding, creating dark corners and cracks, while exposing vulnerable people who rely on darkness as refuge. My friend in college did not want it brighter, she only wanted to move freely without fear. To light everything up would kill the night.

Irvin and I are at the edge, and I feel like I'm leaning back to where we came from. The city looks like a brilliant soup in the bottom of a bowl, and it grays the air around us with photons. The giant LED sphere I'd visited that morning turns blue, green, and red like a marble, far enough away I could reach out and pick it up with two fingers. A mile and a half from Sphere, across the blaze of the Strip, the Luxor's skybeam stabs straight up thousands of feet, a column of light that's been reported by pilots taking off at the LA airport two hundred miles away. The view of civilization beaming its heart out looks like a nervous system sparked to life with arcing bolts of Frankenstein electricity driving nighttime economies, infrastructure moving nonstop. Everything we touch seems to be charged. Where in this city does a person find refuge from the light?

Reclining over Vegas, the constellation Orion is nearly burned out of existence. The distinctive, three-starred belt barely shows through a dishwater sky. Sirius is one of the brightest stars and closest to Earth, a fist-width from Orion's heel, but tonight if I look away, I have trouble finding it again. You could call a starry sky our cosmic commons, and it is reduced to ash by what this city generates. Jupiter is up, greenish, maybe blue, the brightest of all the dots and easiest to find. The planet is in opposition to Earth right now, like seeing the full moon, but it's a full Jupiter, bouncing back as much light as it can to break through this vaporous night. Most stars when I look straight at them, their light dissolves like sugar in a teacup, leaving enough evidence to show something celestial is happening above us but not enough for someone like Ptolemy to sink his teeth into. If this was all we'd been able to see throughout history, we might still be doing math on our fingers and thinking the Earth is flat.

Beneath emergency vehicle sirens and shrieking motorcycles, the city emits a sound like putting your ear to the metal of an air duct, a swarm that doesn't stop coming. It is engines and innumerable motors, heaters on roofs, pipes hissing, power cables singing one continuous note atop another. The boundary we occupy tonight is far quieter than last night, and not nearly as loud as skimming the interstate for the last few hours. We can talk to and hear each other. A strong wind picks up as we dig nuts and jerky out of bags, sitting on little squares of foam pads for cushions as we face Vegas. Facing the other way makes no sense. You don't pull up a seat to a fire and sit with your back to it.

Irvin and I stare like dumb animals. The skybeam shining up from a black glass pyramid at one end of the Strip shoots straight into space, offering a lesser kind of light pollution than the light of Sphere, which sheds in all directions, representing a new stage of human illumination.

"Las Vegas is an attractive nuisance," he says, lifting the term from his Forest Service work, referring to a piece of land that unintentionally invites trouble, luring animals into danger. "We got sucked into it; it's not the goal, it's the distraction," he says not so much to me as the city in front of him.

Imagine a city with its lights turned to a dim glow, just enough to see and little more. Windows on tall buildings are tinted from the inside, the downtown in the nighttime not blinding, but soft, like a downturned gaze. Your other senses engage, perceive more, work a little harder and healthier. Las Vegas has been trying to create a meager but commendable version of this over the last decade. Once a year or so, the Strip holds what it calls "Earth Hour," when a number of major casinos dial back exterior lighting and flashing banners for one hour, which the internet experiences as a bump of hate, comments far and wide about how people didn't come to take selfies in a half-lit megalopolis. Watch crime go up, they warn. Hold onto your purses and wives. The idea behind Earth Hour is acknowledging the cost and waste of energy, a nod to the price of excess. The skybeam at the Luxor now runs at half of the forty-two billion candlepower it was designed for, half of its xenon bulbs turned off, and still it does the job. If I had my way, the trend would keep going, it would accelerate, and it would not be Earth Hour, but Dark Hour, or Dark Night, lights switched to a color more like flame. Emergency workers don't agree. Without proper lighting, blood and antifreeze on the street look the same. In the plus column, constellations would be as regular as nightly news. You'd know Venus from Jupiter the way you know a lily from a rose. I'd argue there'd be less blood on the street, more calmness everywhere. Circadian rhythms would reset, returning to their original, three-billion-year-old position, and your home would be softly lit as if by candles, gently darkening before bed. Imagine the sanity.

This is how the trend spreads, light placement treated with nuance, not a blunt tool to vanquish every shadow, but one for polishing, one for reading, one for city sidewalks, one for porches. The human world is not monolithic, not one kind of light for everything. Artificial light has been found to increase crime. And to decrease crime. And to have no effect whatsoever. Lighting engineers have gone in with half the lumens at urban pinch points and found that people felt just as comfortable. Fixtures were eliminated or repositioned, given warmer color temperatures, or shielded to shine only where needed and not everywhere else. Having the right number of lights at the right level, and not just dumping fixtures at regular intervals but fitting them carefully into their surroundings dramatically reduces how much light we produce. I spoke with an architectural lighting designer who used words like *highly efficient* and *very precise*. He told me finesse with this kind of infrastructure is spreading, cities building master plans around preserving darkness, moonlights for walkways, timers and dimmers raising and lowering intensity based on the time of night and the present need. He said he thinks we've passed peak illumination and our world is gradually darkening, by choice.

I'm abashed to admit I like Las Vegas, plugging myself directly into the human power center. Irvin gets it; he likes it, too. Tomorrow night the urban glow will be farther behind us, the view of it not as commanding. This is our last night of direct eye contact, and it's got me hooked. If I could go back for one more romp in the electrified heart, I'd be tempted. A firefighter I know who offered to help our trek—and loaned us these two bikes—works in the city. He took us out to a strip-mall tiki bar where we entered a manufactured volcanic underworld, music pumping, ceiling made of twinkling diodes arranged to imitate stars, under which bartenders set drinks on fire. Fake meteorites launched and faded over our heads. I got two readings on my meter, 13.85 and 14.45, which I threw away as useless, a lark inside what felt like a torch-lit cavern. One more evening of bars and talking loudly, yelling through music? Why not? Out here, we're sitting in a blue bath of all the lights put together, a luminous, generic vapor, and I'm feeling symptoms of withdrawal.

"The light draws certain animals," Irvin says. "Like a ladybug, a ladybird beetle. They climb naturally to the tip of your finger." He holds up his index finger as if he's got a beetle on it, and he can see, as I do, how the imaginary bug would open its shell and be carried skyward on thin black wings.

"Some animals are just upward bound," he says.

"Positive phototaxis," I say, which is how naturalists sometimes communicate, a classroom for each other.

"Then there are bugs that live under logs, those little darkling beetles," he says, poking a hand into imaginary detritus, going under things. "They're looking for dark," he says. "Rats are a great example. You can catch them by getting them to go into a dark hole. That's what a trap is. They go toward the darkest spot, even if it might kill them."

"Negative phototaxis," I say, thinking that we are a species of both, needing dark no less than light.

"I don't like negative phototaxis," he says. "There must be another word for being drawn *to* the dark. It's not photo, it's the opposite of photo. Attraction to darkness, dark-taxis?"

A word that could fit in this case would be *nyctophilia*, where one finds relief in darkness. From the Greek word *nýx*, which means night, these people are called nyctophiles, and in its extreme this is considered a psychological disorder, fear of light, an intense need for darkness. I don't know if there's a word for what I'm looking for, *astrophiles*, *cosmophiles*, which I think describes most people so it shouldn't be named, it should just be how we are, part of ourselves drawn to the night. Even my friend who suffers from space dread appreciates the night sky, finds relief in it. Between his existential fears, he told me it's one of the most beautiful things a person could see.

Tonight, three of the Seven Sisters, the stars of the Pleiades cluster, are visible enough to suggest the shape of a tiny kite, a diamond with a tail. The North Star, Polaris, is still shy. It's the one that leads mariners circling the Northern Hemisphere, the single star that sits over the pole. I see where it ought to be, but no matter how I stare to the north, it's not there. Twenty stars, maybe thirty are visible, which is a fine start.

Standing crookedly, getting my body upright, I pick up my pad, no bigger than a book cover, and say goodnight. Irvin says the same. I shuffle through a chill wind back to my bike and its island of unpacked gear. He works his way into his bag, putting to bed a hectic day. Mountains at the back of the city shine as if onstage.

BORTLE 7

* * * * * * * * * * *

The entire sky background has a vague, grayish white hue. Strong light sources are evident in all directions. The Milky Way is invisible. M44 or M31 may be glimpsed with the unaided eye but are very indistinct. Clouds are brilliantly lit. Even in moderate-size telescopes, the brightest Messier objects are pale ghosts of their true selves.

* * * * * * * * * * *

BORTLE 7

To see through a grasshopper's eyes, get down and crawl. Use your eyes to tell up from down. These would be five eyes, two big compound eyes taking up much of the head, the other three clustered together above them. These smaller eyes are used solely for distinguishing dark from light, the strongest incoming signals to a grasshopper's stringy brain. Your primary thought is your awareness of polarization—what is up, what is down, lighter and darker. Flying insects orient themselves this way, and knowing what a disoriented bug looks like twitching on its back, you'll want to keep the two sides in order.

A grasshopper is a dart with wings. When they fly en masse, they aim at the brightest place on the horizon, their bull's-eye. A city during the day means nothing, but at night, its brightness makes it stand out sharply against the darker sky, naturally luring grasshoppers as it does most insects. Spiraling to keep light on one side, constantly bending toward it, insects forget everything else. If you were a grasshopper, you would do the same, tumbling with your fellow insects in free fall toward the brightest place.

If you've driven into Vegas, you can understand how a swarm of grasshoppers might converge. From fifty miles out, the Vegas dome looks like a contact lens held at arm's length. Leading the way is a trail of lights, a sodium vapor bulb on a pole outside a barn followed by a gas station, then a well-lit exit off a highway. Cobra-head street lights line up to welcome you like paparazzi, all the air blistered white as the city nears. Interstates gather into billboards that elevate into slabs of LED screens, and then cloverleaves pile up. The number of other grasshoppers around you becomes a swarm.

As grasshoppers, you tend to be quiet and still at night, your species diurnal. Much of your life is solitary; other grasshoppers are encountered mostly by accident. But artificial light has changed this. The swarming mechanism is flipped on. The thoracic part of your thinking structure, up near the eyes, the center of locomotion, is flushed with serotonin and turned up high, which usually happens only during daylight. Every grasshopper around you reacts the same as if you were all on ecstasy. Humans also produce serotonin when exposed to blue wavelengths, and also while on the drug ecstasy. If you've been there yourself as a human, you have some idea what it feels like to be a grasshopper. As your velum wings shake the nighttime air, fellow grasshoppers are experiencing the same, all going joyfully mad with light.

If you're not distracted by a stadium or stranded at the battery of fluorescents in front of a convenience store, you'll keep flying toward the center, the brightest of horizons. Who can remember the long dark desert that led here, the mountains standing under luxuriant night? Certainly not a grasshopper. You have always used light and dark to execute maneuvers and to know your travel speed and the distance you've covered. Now you know nothing at all, which must feel like knowing everything, lost in radiance.

When an estimated forty-eight million pallid-winged grasshoppers converged on Las Vegas in the summer of 2019, they came from as far as sixty miles away, flying from all directions, from ground level to a mile up in the air. Radars that track storms picked up clouds of insects with a confluence that looked galactic, each spiral arm shaped by incoming highways, interstates, and gaps in the mountains where Vegas had line of sight on the grasshoppers. In the center, at the white heart of the galaxy, grasshoppers wandered in every direction, no longer a swarm in motion but an event horizon, the sidewalks crawling, people running and waving their hands around their heads.

If lights had been switched off, the swarm would have fallen. Night replaces serotonin with melatonin, and the transformation would be swift in these small bodies. The ecstasy would end. You'd find a place to tuck in and hold fast till sunrise.

Eventually, the 2019 swarm died off, though it took days. Grasshoppers could not survive this kind of outpouring, littering streets and cars with their bodies, millions upon millions crushed into pavement under shoes. Workers with sprayers peeled their remains into gutters.

Morning haze sits cold on the city, temperatures blown in around freezing. The romance of night is over, replaced by an opaque curdle, a broth of hydrocarbons, ozone, and acidified aerosols mixed with cigarette smoke and exhaust pipes over gray and shimmering Vegas. A late autumn inversion has settled in, and we're camped just high enough to see across its roof. Lights that would draw swarms of flying creatures have been replaced by the sun coming up from behind the mountains like a nuclear blast.

Daytime is not as attractive in this city. The word ugly comes to mind. Pollution levels change in the absence of darkness. Burning fossil fuels release nitrogen oxide and volatile organic compounds that interact with sunlight to create ground-level ozone, which is smog. At night, the chemistry reverses and ozone is destroyed. Without sunlight, an oxidant forms in the air that reacts with and neutralizes nitrogen oxide, decreasing the smog. In the absence of dark, smog stacks on top of itself without cessation, which makes Vegas look like a morning hangover.

I'm grouchy, irritated from lack of sleep. Wind blew down the barrel of my bag all night, no matter how tightly I cinched the draw. Sun is in my eyes, and my legs feel like they've been beaten after yesterday's ride. My scalp itches from being buried in a wool cap. My circadian clock didn't go off, and I'm pissed. I should have been out of my bag hours ago. Instead, I'm sitting up in a down and nylon sleeve, and the first word out of my mouth is a curse.

I missed dawn altogether. The whole point of being out here is to carefully note the coming and going of night, and I missed Venus passing behind the crescent moon, an occultation I'd been excited to witness. This transit of celestial bodies is a long-distance eclipse that happens two or three times most years, which can be seen if you're in the right place at the right time. Venus slips behind the lit-up crescent and an hour later pops from behind the moon's dark side like a lustrous seed. But every time I tried to wake up, I pulled my bag tighter, half asleep and mumbling. I told myself I'd stir in time to see Venus and the moon touching, but I'm too late and sunrise has washed out both. Tomorrow, they'll be farther apart, the moment gone.

Unlike de Mairan's mimosa plant, which opens and closes with clockwork regularity, I'm only now peeling out of my bag and into morning clothes. The desert around camp is knifed with Joshua trees ten feet tall. Irvin is still in his bag, hazy from night wind. The city's edge is an ejecta blanket of waste and half-roads going nowhere, forgotten furnishings dumped and wind-rotted, half-welded objects left on the ground, souvenirs of ideas that never panned out. Stained rips of plywood that nobody wanted lie twenty feet from where I slept. This ring of detritus continues for eighty miles, all the way around Vegas. A piece of luggage, probably stolen from a tour bus, lies open in a foxhole where the city's direct light can't reach. A thief had rummaged through it, a coyote scrounging in a carcass.

Instead of coffee, I walk to this strewn luggage, finding signs of what was supposed to be a woman's vacation bleaching on rocky ground. A sweatshirt with hearts on it has turned crisp in the sun. A few pairs of high-heeled shoes point up like caltrops. I'm a desert kid, having grown up partly around Phoenix, the valley of my birth, where I've made myself comfortable with despairing, junked-out arroyo roads and shot-up furniture at the edge of town. I learned that torn-open box springs are popular for black widows, with their moon-like egg sacs nesting in the coils, and scorpions lie flat underneath moldering folds of fabric. The desert won't let us hide from our nastiness. I move from one station of junk to the next as if through a church, kicking over the prayer book of a computer hard drive perforated from target practice, taking communion from a TV shot through its face. We do this with real estate no one cares about, the Holy Rubbish Fellowship, the Epiphanic Chapel of Detritus. The land has died for our sins.

Inside the rut of a motorbike lies the crushed, desiccated remains of a desert tortoise, the few pieces ants and ravens haven't picked off—parts of a single leg and hexagonal pieces of shell hinged together like parched leather. With its big rubber lugs, the bike's tire had dug through the ground's surface, opening pale dust where the throttle got a twist to go faster, a mark still evident a year or more after it was made. Hit directly, the tortoise must have popped like a gourd.

Irvin and I get down on the ground with what's left of the animal, Irvin taking tiny leg bones in his fingers, a few scales of foot skin still intact, blunt little claws.

"Tortoise medicine," he says, arranging the bones on a limestone cobble. As if reciting the credo of the tortoise, he says, "Move slow, make distance."

"You think someone aimed for it?" I ask.

"I'd like to think they didn't," he says.

Irvin's wife is also a biologist, and she now works for the Federal Communications Commission, where she considers the impacts of communication infrastructure on the environment, mainly how warning lights on radio towers affect birds. Her first fieldwork thirty years ago was endangered tortoise surveys outside of Las Vegas, and decades later she fondly remembers the study as one of the best times in her life: walking the dry Mojave over hill and dale, seeing and recording a tortoise on rare occasions, mostly encountering a gigantic sky and desert to match. Later, she worked on environmental impact studies for a solar tower in the Mojave, numbering and tracking endangered tortoises in the lead of development. You might have seen these towers while flying over the far Southwest. They're called concentrating solar plants, rings of ten thousand mirrors focusing sunlight onto a center point, superheating a core of molten salt elevated onto a tower and tapped day and night for electricity. The installations look like suns on Earth, globules of pure light that could set ships on fire. From tens of thousands of feet in the air, peering through the oval window of an airplane, I've seen them below like the sun focused through a magnifying glass, burning a hot hole just above the ground like an atom bomb.

As Irvin readies gear, cinching last-minute problems with his bags, I drift back through the sunbaked suitcase lying open, its stolen belongings scattered as if crash-landed. It would be heartening if some sort of balance were being kept, and the original owner of the suitcase had paid a small debt by losing her luggage, a grain of karma removed from her scale. That's what I wish for her, seeing the makeup she'd brought and her nightclub dress, knee-length with polka dots, the joy she planned to have. There's no paper, no personal ID. She probably wouldn't want to be contacted, told that a stranger had rifled through her belongings and decided most were useless.

When Irvin has his gear buckled up, I leave this minor disaster and we bike away from the scene. I feel like we're dragging tin cans of civilization behind us on a string, clattering as we get off the dead-end gravel road and back onto smooth pavement.

Maybe it's my disrupted circadian hormones or lack of sleep, but a foul mood has settled in, not how I wanted to start this quest. Cut off from cocktails and loud bars, that could be it. I've got a headache, and it doesn't take long before I'm sick of pumping through endless neighborhoods looking for a way out. Escaping

Vegas is like getting through a maze. You're not supposed to leave. Subdivisions are named like New Hampshire real estate colonies—Franklin Park, Hampton Glen, Cambridge at Providence—crowded oddly into the Mojave Desert. Irvin's got his command center going between handlebars, phone screen showing a map where some of these subdivisions don't yet exist, yet there they are in front of us, blocking the way. We turn around a few times. There are gates and new cul-de-sacs, a school where there wasn't one before.

We finally break out along a high-tension powerline, taking an access road that leads past enormous flood control structures that look like classic Egyptian architecture followed by a buzzing compound of fenced-in towers and cables sending electricity from Hoover Dam to far-off places. This long-haul power system causes the air to crackle overhead, a kind of music, an atmospheric drone. Sixteen high-voltage powerlines stacked over our heads seem like overkill, but somebody needs all this electricity. The dam isn't far from Vegas, wedged into a dark, rocky canyon along the Colorado River. Some of the hydropower it produces stays local, more goes to Arizona, and most is sent to California. We've reached an infrastructure node to see us out of the city, a spider web woven across hundreds of miles. I've heard there's no scientific proof heavy electromagnetic fields like this have health effects, but I feel lightheaded, which might be the faint awareness that electricity is traveling just under the speed of light, hardly a blink to get it from here to the light switch turned on in Los Angeles. A cell tower is crammed into the corner of the substation with receivers and transmitters pointed every direction, sending and receiving invisible waves. We roll along the perimeter fence as our tires press small rocks into the dust. Powerlines cross a clear sky, and above them floats a lighter weave of contrails from jets coming and going. What a busy world we've made. It makes you dizzy.

One of the major lines aims due west, held aloft by a file

of metal towers marching across the Mojave toward California. We follow this for a short distance and then turn northerly along a subroutine of wooden poles carrying a smaller load out to the Las Vegas Paiute Reservation. Pole skin is burnt and splintered in the sun, which is where our woes begin. The road scrapped underneath this line is all we've got and it's not good. Powerline roads are notorious, designed for inconvenient travel. Motorbikers don't like them, preferring to gun across open desert, which we can't do because we lack the mechanical advantage, and we're weighed down heavily with water and gear. We need what little road there is. Several weeks ago, thunderstorms blew out long sections of it, and washes crossing at ninety degrees were freshly coffered with rocks that no one has driven on to pack down.

For lunch, we sit on the ground with hunks of cheese and salami sliced with a knife while our bikes lean against a shaved wooden power pole. "Color of the sky?" I ask as I scribble in a small red notebook.

"Baby blue," says Irvin. "A little hazy with particulates from the wind."

"Would you say half Earth, half sky?" I ask.

He looks around us at the circle of a serrated horizon and answers, "Fifty-five percent Earth, forty-five percent sky."

The substation is far enough behind us it looks like a distant shipwreck. I peer up at the deeper blue directly above. If you stare long enough, it appears almost black, as if you're seeing off the planet. "Feels like you can see space," I say.

Irvin glances up, stares, then goes back to eating. "Thinner atmosphere at the zenith," he says. "Fewer parts per million to see through."

He's a scientist through and through, the most curious variety. We've trekked in dry places to find water, eaten whatever we could for sustenance, and kept notebooks of Latin names for plants and animals. Two scrappy, hungry naturalists thirty years ago, we haven't changed at heart, hard to talk about anything but Earth and sky together. We load back onto bikes, pulling zippers and straps, and push off as if setting across a great body of water.

You don't touch your brakes on a road like this, needing momentum at every spin of gravel. The blue of the sky ahead mixes with wind haze, giving it a color of sapphires buried in sawdust. The closer you pay attention, the more color you see. If the sky were a paint tube, it would be labeled *hayseed blue* or *exhausted topaz*. The land we're entering is mainly populated with creosote bushes that live up to ten thousand years and Joshua trees, which top out at five hundred. Mostly, it's air, spaces in between, and signs of life here and there. With its depressions and ridgelines, the longer view looks like the face of Venus, but more orderly, with musical ripples of mountain ranges and basins on tectonic repeat, one sunken after the next. The mountain ranges have spent millions of years burying themselves in eroded spall, forming plains of broken rock thousands of feet deep, debris fans called bajadas. These bajadas overlap like colossal clamshells beneath the mountains, and the road keeps a perfectly straight line across them, no give or take, just a plow mark, damn the terrain.

I see Irvin walking a couple hundred feet ahead of me, struggling to push his bike up a steep, crumbling bank. I grind into my pedals to gather momentum. I'm not what you'd call a lithe flower of a man, more like a bear on a bicycle, grunting hard to gain speed down the side of a gully into a minefield of water sculptures left by floods. Tires swerve through bays of soft gravel and knotted heads of flood-stripped creosote bushes. Ducking, dodging, I promise myself I'm not walking up the other side, where Irvin's now catching his breath at the top. He's looking dusty and roughed up, as if he'd crashed. This is why travel in twos works well. When one hits a problem, the other is warned, and I slither with all the speed I can muster to get up the other side with rocks pinging off my spokes. Tires grab the cut bank and I'm up on all fours pumping, pumping, hissing obscenities through my teeth, thinking I might top out when the combined mass of myself and my belongings crashes to the ground in slow motion. My shoulder and hips plow into rocks. I sputter, curse, and lie for a moment under the weight of my bike. Irvin is giving me a look; he toppled in the same place.

I'm not sure our trip will work. I don't say this aloud, but we're moving at two miles per hour, three at times, no quicker than walking. Unless we want to hop the death trap of concrete barriers and guardrails along the highway a third of a mile away—which we don't—this is the only route to get to the next road on the map, a longer, wilder one without power poles. From there, we should be delivered from the farther wrack line of Vegas. The object is to document the retreat of light and the coming of true, Earthly darkness. At this point, we've hardly turned a page.

Tomorrow, we are supposed to start a long stretch between resupply points: no towns, no lights, no nothing. I'd been calculating odds of us reaching water caches and putting the lights of Vegas permanently behind us, but now I'm scouting out front, biking the rollercoaster line of this road and not thinking days ahead. My mind zeroes in on what's immediately in front of me, holes and rocks bigger than grapefruits, front tire dodging around obstacles that hammer shock absorbers on the forks. The heavy rear doesn't dodge as easily, hitting behind me everything I'm trying to get around, sandpits and flood cobbles, pea gravel parting like water. With no rear suspension, gears shudder at every lump in the way.

You would think along this straight road you'd see somebody coming for miles, but you can't. The land undulates, hiding half of itself over every rise. I don't see the walker until I look ahead and pick out a solitary figure on foot a quarter mile away. Who would be on foot this far out into pretty much nowhere, on the far side of Southern Paiute land now half a mile from a public right-of-way four-lane with medians and nonstop driving? The person goes in and out of view as we drop into washes and haul ourselves over the next rise. He's the height of an average male, and he's carrying something in one hand, something larger than a human head.

Irvin behind me feels a similar trepidation, biking through a Breaking Bad desert, No Man's Land, imagining a delirious fool ahead hopped up on meth, someone who chose not to get a ride but came into the city out of the desert on foot. Who would do that? Irvin's glad he's in the rear.

Over the subsequent rise, I see it's a man. His green jacket is zipped to his neck, and his sweatpants are tarnished. The object held by one hand remains a mystery. I pull up to him, and I must look like I'm on outer-space safari, sunglasses under my helmet and a big bandana draped to keep the sun off my neck. The man looks to be in his late thirties, weathered enough to hide his age, jacket pocked with wear holes, a running shoe emblem on his black ball cap. I was hoping for a Paiute, a local, so we could get advice, maybe a better side road, but he's a white man coming from who knows where. He has no pack or satchel, only a bundle in his left hand, which turns out to be a ratty American flag tied into a knot, the knot used as a handle. Inside it, he carries everything he has, no bigger than an armful, not much. He's squinting at me because I'm in the south with the midday sun at forehead level, so I walk the bike forward and say hello. He says hello right back—a disarming voice, like it's no surprise to see another space traveler out here. He asks where we're heading, and I say we're avoiding the highway on our way north. He's missing a front tooth and hasn't shaved in a couple of weeks. He says the road behind him sucks, full of washouts. But he doesn't seem frustrated. He has the purposeful air of a pilgrim. When I ask where he's coming from, he says, "Death Valley."

My mind goes to California, jumping over five, maybe five and a half mountain ranges to get there, and everything between here and there is one of the drier stretches of American desert.

"Death Valley?" I say. "That's a long way."

"I know," he says.

I point north where we'll cross the highway many miles off, and beyond that, a gateway opening between mountain ranges, distances hard to judge—thirty or forty miles by line of sight. He says we've got several more miles of chop, and there's a road off to a Chevron station. "Great place to get candy," he says.

"Where're you heading?" I ask, and he says, "Las Vegas."

"It's right over that horizon," I jerk my thumb behind me. "Twenty miles to downtown, you're almost there."

Irvin pulls up and joins the meeting. "He says the road sucks from here," I say.

Irvin laughs and says, "Excellent."

I assume the man's been camping, maybe spent the night in the filling station bathroom. As close to the city as he would have been last night, he would have seen an ivory lid for a sky. Maybe he got a ride, and was dropped off at the filling station so he could walk the last stretch alone, coming into the city unobtrusively. We're moving retrograde to each other, so we're not staying long enough to find out.

I ask about his water supply. He says he hasn't had any since the Chevron. Without getting off my bike, I pull a bottle from the frame, and he uncrunches a plastic bottle from his bundle. I fill it with half a quart. He tips his lips to it and eyes me from under his ball cap as I take shots with my phone of the horizon, the road, him holding the water, documenting what is encountered along the way. He empties the bottle in one shot, and when I ask if he wants more, he says he's good and thanks us both, crunching the bottle back into his bundle.

"I've got candy," he offers. "Gummy bears, Skittles." He seems enthused about the offer. Getting to the Chevron seems to have made his day. Candy is some of the cheapest, quickest calories you can buy, rocket fuel to Vegas. By end of day tomorrow, I could see him as one of the unhoused many on the street, and maybe the hectic city will drive him to angry shouting at the air, a natural response to urban pressure. Or he'll amble back into his life, unlock the front door after a walkabout, and sit down on his own couch. We don't know his story. We decline his candy offer, not wanting to tap his few supplies, and the conversation is left there. He continues toward Vegas with his flag bundle, and Irvin and I ride the other way.

Every highway, interstate, and gas station is a beacon leading to the nucleus. The positive phototaxic grasshopper follows one bright marker to the next, leading into the electric-blue-green infinity. Along with insects come birds and bats. The migration can turn into a flying maelstrom. Being blind as a bat does not mean blind to overall light conditions. Bats have the same kinds of cone cell structures in their eyes as birds, fish, amphibians, and reptiles; they keep them focused on polarity, the most rudimentary orientation they know. Echolocation is for catching prey and avoiding obstacles, but a bat still has eyes to see the light.

Navigation by polarity—one direction being light, the other dark—is called a sky compass. Butterflies, honeybees, and assortments of beetles use this compass where light patterns and locations of sun and moon are more reliable than physical landmarks, so they come first in the brain's navigational hierarchy. Birds fall even more easily under the spell, drawn away from migratory paths and flocking to cities where, at a certain point, everything is equally lit, and there is no more polarity, no more up or down. By then, it's too late.

The night of September 11, 2002, I witnessed an extreme trapping event in Lower Manhattan when I walked with a friend toward the twin light beams projected as a memorial from Ground Zero where the World Trade Center towers had fallen the year before. We bustled through the crowd to the center of the action where batteries of eighty-eight hot-white 7,000-watt xenon bulbs sent up a pair of columns four miles high, and birds crowded into the blaze as if pulled by a magnet. There must have been thousands inside the columns, every kind of flight pattern, swooping raptors, soaring gulls, the swift flutter of shorebirds. There were perching songbirds and the broad wingspans of high ocean fliers. Their inflamed movements reflected in windows of surrounding buildings as if the skies were clogged by the aviary end of evolution. There were also bats flittering and the quicker motions of insects, plus droves of tens of thousands of two-legged humans on the ground as if an anthill had been kicked.

We were there for vigil and remembrance while the birds were more intimately overwhelmed. Many would die by exhausting themselves in their wild circling or from smashing into nearby windows, while those that survived would make little or no progress toward their ultimate destinations of faraway marshes, woods, coasts, meadows, dunes. They were stuck here going round and round.

Shine a light along the edge of a lake at night, and if you're in the right spot, hundreds of tiny fish will break the surface like popcorn. In a split second, their navigation flips, and they'll do anything to reach the light, even if it kills them.

Turtle hatchlings on a beach head for the sea because it reflects the moon or starry sky, not the black earth behind them. But if that black earth is artificially lit, they'll head in that direction instead.

Birds might have it the worst. Their pineal gland, which connects the endocrine system to the perception of light, is much more sensitive than it is in humans and most animals, meaning light has more of a full-body effect, shining through their bones and triggering internal photoreceptors. Their skulls are thin enough to let light into the brain, and photoreceptors have evolved within their brains, acting as a soft third eye.

Cities are unkind to birds unless they're resilient crows or pigeons or house sparrows finding some haven or park to call home. The most significant bird migration corridors in the world cross through major cities that wreak havoc by bringing them into a mostly unfavorable habitat where risks are high, and windows are killing fields, leaving feathered bodies on the sidewalks. New York City lies along the Atlantic Flyway, one of the more prominent global bird migration routes, and it is highly active in September when the two beams of this memorial go up annually. The light beams are poles around which they cannot help circling, with the orientation of above and below packaged into a single, ecstatic axis. Years after that first memorial, these two pillars of light would be shut down for twenty minutes at a time once the volume of fliers reached critical mass, as called in by Audubon Society observers on the ground. A radar bounce over the memorial picked up approximately five hundred birds after the lights were turned off. When they were turned back on twenty minutes later, almost sixteen thousand birds poured back in.

Those that make it through the night will be subject to hormonal chaos, with a reduced chance of survival from having light bleeding through their systems, shot into their bodies like X-rays. It would be unfair to say the memorial alone causes this. It comes from every light turned upward and reflected off pavement or grass, the sum of it all turning the sky into a puzzle birds can't solve. It happens in every city and, to a lesser degree, every town. They see the light far away and head toward it.

The solution is to darken what we can and use lights colored more like flame and less like the sun. Tone down those blue headlights on cars, draw shades on windows, and shield electrified signs so they're only seen by those who were meant to see them. Install motion sensors so that empty lots aren't lit at every hour. Put dimmers on anything we can. Give our eyes a rest, all of them.

The berserk spectacle with the birds I witnessed in Manhattan is the apotheosis of what can happen anywhere light shines at night. From the birds' point of view, that experience must have looked angelic in a hellish way, as if war was being waged in heaven, everything turned upside down and falling. They don't die just because they smack into windows, or into each other, or spiral to the ground from exhaustion; they die because this volume of light, the volume most of us live with night to night, causes the general dampening of their ability to survive and reproduce.

Jenny Ouyang, a professor and ecologist at the University of Nevada, Reno, examines what artificial light does to birds, and she's seen effects across the board, from behavioral changes to disease. "In urban areas, birds will sing earlier because there's light at night," Ouyang told me. "They'll start reproducing earlier in the season or not at the right time. Light's telling them it's time to go, and they go and have a clutch of eggs and babies. But there aren't the insects to feed on, to feed their babies."

Urbanization is a fast and widespread way to change the surface of the Earth, and Ouyang sees the light that comes along with it as a toxin that, if unchecked, spreads rampantly. Birds are the canaries in the coal mine, so to speak. Their awareness of when to mate, feed, nest, and migrate is driven by photoreceptors inside their brains where light pushes hormonal buttons. By flooding them with light, we are constantly resetting their biological systems.

Ouyang said, "As the world becomes more urban with more people and more light, I wanted to do research asking, 'What are the effects of this pollutant, besides my aesthetically nostalgic feeling of enjoying the night sky?'"

She heads the Ouyang Lab at the University's Department of Biology. Its mission is to study how animals adapt to changing environments, particularly the changes that we drive, working with heavy metals and contaminants that are nearly impossible to extract from the environment—endocrine disrupters requiring industrial removal techniques. Meanwhile, light pollution, she said, is a simple matter of turning off a switch, or at least turning one down. "Of all the pollutants," she told me, "I feel like this is one of the easier to solve."

Ouyang's early childhood was in China where she had little to no view of the heavens, much of it spent in Xi'an, the capital of the landlocked Shaanxi Province and currently at the top of China's list of some of the country's worst urban air pollution. The population was around three million when she lived there from 1985 to 1995, at the beginning of accelerated LED technology, and now it's thirteen million. She remembers streets crowded with bicycles, and when she returned to visit in 2018, she found the bikes had been mostly replaced by cars, making it harder to breathe, and the city was brighter than she could have imagined. As a child, there were no stars for her, and now the night sky is an even blanker slate. Still, she grew up singing a nursery rhyme most will find familiar. She sang it over the phone to me: "Yi shan yi shan, liang jing jing." The simple translation is "twinkle, twinkle, little star." In school, she learned Li Bai's poems from the eighth century, many of which addressed the moon and stars, and, like kids her age around the world, she learned to draw the same five-pointed star with five quick strokes. To her, stars seemed like mythical objects that did not exist in the real world—a twinkling in a fabled sky.

At nine, her family moved to San Luis Obispo, California, where you might imagine it to be darker than in one of China's bigger cities, but being near Los Angeles it was simply another over-lit hotspot. She saw a few more stars, but not many, hardly a reason to lift her gaze. At age twenty, she had yet to see the Milky Way, and she was a biology undergrad taking an ecology class at the University of California, Irvine. The class went to Joshua Tree National Park in the Mojave Desert for a day of fieldwork, followed by a night of camping where two faculty and about thirty students sat outside watching the night come on. The transition, with its shifting colors, bewitched her. As stars rolled out, she had trouble remembering how it happened; they must have come on one by one, but each time she looked, there'd be a hundred more. They filled the sky. Her voice faltered as she recalled seeing the Milky Way for the first time.

"I think I cried," Ouyang said. Then she corrected herself. "I know I cried."

Shadows cast ten miles long as the last sun tucks between ridges and mountain tops. Dusk falls faster on our basin side and slower on the other side, the sunset watched not by looking toward it but by looking in the opposite direction toward blood-orange peaks. End-of-day light climbs the highest summits till it's airborne and we fall into the shadow of the Earth. My internal compass starts up, shoulders relaxing as I settle into cardinal directions, brain tingling with orientation.

My ass is sore from banging around all day on a broomstick. Is this spade-shaped taint-basher all we could think up for a bike seat design? At least I'm not crabbed over a keyboard, eyes two feet from a retina-splitting monitor, spinal column sinking toward the floor in a chair. It's why I come out here, to shake myself off, cobwebs coughed out, pupils stretched as if waking. Nothing here is designed for us or our bicycles, certainly not this powerline road and not these Joshua trees, which don't look like trees but like beasts occupied with their own spike-headed business. This is a definition of liberty, being rattled and jarred to pieces without anyone else's concern.

Irvin, wearing a warm hat and layers of coats, comes back from a walk up the wash, clutching woody flood debris in both hands, a husk of a Joshua tree appendage, and tangled roots that died months ago. He's got a wide-eyed half-smile on his face, a man back from a fine end-of-the-day walk. "The channels have all been reshaped by this last flood event," he says. "There's plenty of wood to burn."

I'd said no fires on this trip, wanting to keep it night-sky-only, but the temperature is already dropping, so I say fire sounds perfect. The wood and crunched-grass kindling is dry enough he gets it started with a single lighter flick. With a few huffs and puffs, his face close to the ground, he gets a flame going and we both add sticks, snapping them in half one at a time. Fire has a redder wavelength than most artificial lights. The red end of the spectrum comes in long, languid wavelengths, which is why you can look up from a campfire and still see the stars.

They come out slowly through a margarita meltwater sky. More of Orion is visible than last night. The hunter constellation flaunts his scabbard or whatever is said to hang below that sideways belt of his. The red-eyed V of Taurus shows itself through the light-swamp. The Seven Sisters of the Pleiades are still three.

The language of the night sky is easy to get back into, learning to identify a few constellations for reference, following the pointer stars of the Big Dipper to find the North Star. Take a picture of where the sun sets from the same place over weeks. Stand a stick in the ground and note shadows as they turn. Realize the greater spheres wheeling around us.

What helps is getting a particular star under your belt. Pick one that catches your eye and see where it's going. Learn its class, its size, and its distance in light years. Find this star when you're unsure what to think of life. Tell it a secret. Wish on it. If it disappears for a season or two, you'll be pleasantly surprised the first time you see it come back into view. If it turns out to be a planet instead of a star—Jupiter and Venus are the brightest—then find it every few nights and see where it moves. You'll notice it's on a different plan than the stars behind it, which is why the Greeks called them wandering stars.

There are other techniques of awareness. As much as anyone I suppose, I believe horoscopes. Sure, it could be relevant where celestial bodies lie when a person is born, equipotential lines of gravity and light plucking invisible threads, causing us to look up and not know why. I have my doubts about what Taurus will experience today, but I'm willing to entertain the notion, like hanging onto the fortune from a cookie for being spot on. If nothing else, astrology is a way of sending our imaginations upward and seeing what Ptolemy saw, what our many ancestors lived with, the sky being more than a pretty picture. Knowing the sign you were born under and the house that held your birth moon is a formality one should be familiar with. Taking notice is a matter of respect since the heavens have been over us for so long, ancestors in themselves.

The night sky is no simple atlas. It is a machine with spinning rotors and jewels. It doesn't need to be memorized for it to keep going. You don't have to know the names of stars or constellations or what personality is bound to which sign. Respect can be nothing more than a glance, looking up and recognizing a greater scale at work.

Our heads are tipped up more than they'd been the night before. The general plane of visibility is rising. We're set back from the four-lane where a river of headlights runs southbound for Vegas, and if drivers see us at all, which they don't, we're a flicker in the corner of the eye, something they're not quite sure they saw. More traffic is coming into the city, significantly more than what's going out. Vegas must be building toward critical mass. Irvin says it's the race, ten days away now, and he's probably right, a bump of 300,000 people estimated for the Grand Prix, coming with a $1.2 billion flush in the local economy. That's what we're seeing, jets lining up a dozen at a time to get into the airport and back out. Look down on this from space, bounce radars off cars and planes, and Vegas resembles a hive, a writhing mass of increasing light.

We're too far out in the folds of bajadas and washes, curved around the edge of a mountain range, to get a line of sight on the city. Yet it is everywhere: Three-quarters of the sky is light-fog. That last quarter in the north is where darkness creeps in, outer space leaking through in the direction we're heading.

I went to high school in Phoenix in the 1980s, and this is the distance from the city I'd drive with my date to park and swap hot breath on the bench seat of my dad's truck. We'd get out and walk amongst saguaros as the sky glittered with stars, Orion as strong as ever. My observation is anecdotal, but this far outside a similarly sized desert metropolis four decades ago, the artificial light was more forgiving, not this platinum gleam. We wouldn't have been making out in a front seat in this kind of light. From my own limited perspective, something has changed. We've moved the night sky farther away.

Our fire goes out, smothered in gravel and dust, burned down to a cup and a half of fine ash at the bottom of the wash. Irvin is wearing flip-flops, the rest of his body bundled warmly in the crispness. The wind has stopped, and a cold river of air flows down from the mountains, moving so slowly it could hardly turn a feather. A chill rises like water, first to our knees, then shoulders, then over our heads.

I stand with my hand in the air, with the SQM device raised so it won't pick up backscatter from my clothes. I am the Statue of Luminosity, casting a shadow from Vegas. There's no Milky Way; I can see where its powder should scatter across the expanse, but the space is empty. Flashing radio towers blink out of sync across the desert tens of miles away. I feel a little like I'm floating, gravity softened slightly, this new pull coming from above and not below. Fifteen minutes of readings get me to a magnitude 18.9, not much of a nudge from yesterday, hardly a complete step through that airlock and into space. The meter takes bites out of the visible spectrum, and I won't pretend to understand the arc seconds involved in its readings, but a number offers a baseline. The darker the night becomes, the higher the number will go, and tomorrow, we'll break 19.

I rerun distances in my head. We're biking slower than planned, and it's also brighter than I expected and ten degrees colder than forecasted. In the morning, we'll get off this powerline road and make a break for wilder country, hopefully picking up miles to get ourselves to the next Bortle.

My thighs burn from the day, and when I shimmy into my sleeping bag, the lactate pools in my muscles and I point my feet up and down to keep from cramping. Above our camp, a big matriarch Joshua tree stabs the pewter haze with shocking black daggers. Shivering, not moving, we both hold onto pockets of warm air around our bodies. Irvin snores. I hear him on the other side of the pronged Joshua tree where our bikes are pitched. I snore, too, and he can hear me.

Neither of us is snoring when I wake and dig a hole out of my hood with a finger. He might be awake, too, but I don't say anything. By three in the morning, most of the Big Dipper has swung around itself like the hands of a clock. I can only see four of its brightest seven stars. A thumbtack hole of Jupiter is heading west, soon to set. I lie awake, listening to the streaking of the highway miles off. Semitrucks gear down around a curve, and above that, I pick up another sound like tinnitus, only it's not my ears. Twenty miles from downtown, ten from the city limits, the rumble of life in Vegas is audible and its light takes up most of the sky.

There's no crunch to my bag, no frost other than a slim ring around my breathing hole. I brought a tent for storms, and Irvin has a waterproof bivvy and a concoction of tarps. But we use neither. It's better to set up in the open, nothing between us and everything else.

BORTLE 6

* * * * * * * * * * *

No trace of the zodiacal light can be seen, even on the best nights. Any indications of the Milky Way are apparent only toward the zenith. The sky within 35° of the horizon glows grayish white. Clouds anywhere in the sky appear fairly bright. You have no trouble seeing eyepieces and telescope accessories on an observing table.

* * * * * * * * * * *

BORTLE 6

Just short of dawn I wake rested, eyes wide as the curtains begin to part. John Steinbeck called this "the hour of the pearl," describing it as "the interval between day and night when time stops and examines itself." Closer to Vegas, it is the hour of onion skin. If there's any pearl this morning, it is a veneer of colors washed across the skyline, and without much ceremony, night falls off the horizon and dayshine takes over. Time doesn't have much time for examination. The sun clears the mountains and we pause packing camp from the base of a Joshua tree as blonde light covers everything, running down tilted shields of alluvial plains. We return to rigging, tightening, and tuning after yesterday rattled us apart.

Back on the road, we face a few rugged miles of powerline choss, and then a spur takes us to the four-lane highway where we time cars and punch straight across, buzzing the median. Half a mile on the other side is a water cache we buried. Topped off, we connect to a long-shot dirt road that leads into open desert. Outside of tire noise, there's only the quiet of a daytime Bortle 6, noise and light seeming to subside together. There are no power poles, no traffic; this is a motor vehicle route meant for trucks and Jeeps and such, and it comes with warnings that Search and Rescue would prefer you check before driving seventy miles from one end to the other. Stranded drivers have been unable to call for help. None have perished to date, but an announcement from the Desert

National Wildlife Refuge Complex to all motorheads in the vicinity reads: "We cannot overstate the hazards drivers will encounter along this route."

Biking is not the same. Our plan is a sort of being stranded, grinding our way up a rock-crackled slope that rises for miles and out of sight, three days to the next water cache. Driving, we'd be across it in half a day if we didn't linger. Not being summer makes all the difference. A temperature of 115 would have immobilized us by now. If you've relied on the midday shade of a Joshua tree, you understand the headachy unpleasantness of lying belly up and moving every ten minutes to stay out of the sun. That time of year, shade means next to nothing. If not direct solar heat, you get radiation from the ground as it shines like a car hood. November is a fine contrast at 82 degrees, down to freezing at night.

This road is far better than the powerline, and still we're banging through boneyards of cobbles, chattering on washboards, and going suddenly quiet with a puff of tires skimming into blow sand. The maps I brought are torn from a paper atlas, pages folded into my gear. Irvin has his panel of systems and a rolled-out solar panel strapped to his tail to keep the tracking gear and his helmet-mounted camera powered. I'm thankful he's on navigation, talking with satellites. Between the two of us, we know where we're going. I check maps every morning and night, and he's got maps downloaded. After I've exhausted my brain on lines of sight, I ask him where we are. He'll calculate, tap the screen, and give me a number: seventy-three miles to our next cache, seventeen miles from where we started this morning.

Rising along the incline of a bajada two thousand feet tall and ten miles across, I work for an hour to catch up with him. Joshua trees look like pilgrims on their way somewhere, all leaning in the same direction as if marching to the city. When I come up by his side, we hardly look at each other, pedals working like lazy windmills, no downhill on this part of the slope. I ask if his rear feels like it's being beaten with a hammer. Irvin looks down at the passing ground, not wanting to think about my question. He was hoping after an hour the first words out of my mouth would be something more profound. He thinks for a moment and says he can't decide if it's his legs or his ass that hurts more, and the thought causes him to stop, and I stop alongside him. Crunch of gravel ceases. There's no sound, not a note. He gets off his bike and as he starts walking it ahead, taking a break but still making distance, he says, "My ass hurts more."

It's not navigation when you have a road. The road does the brain work. I'd thought of inviting someone who knew how to backcountry bike, giving us something to strive for, a lead to follow, but I was afraid it would end up like a cardio workout with someone calling to Irvin and me, *you can make it, you're almost there!*—something we'd never say to each other. We're moving at the right pace, a Bortle per night till we reach the top or the bottom, depending on how you see it. We're in fine enough shape. Irvin can run a wildland firefighter's pack test, the weight and size equivalent of five gallons of water, one hose pack, and a chainsaw with fuel for a mile in 15 minutes or less. After walking half an hour with our bikes, listening to our steps, we mount again and tires catch at the first pedal strokes. Handlebars jerk and twist between softball-sized cobbles. Gear shudders. The road draws in my eye and the brain turns reptilian as I stare in front of the front tire, counting rocks, no real need to navigate.

When I remember there's a sky, I lift my head and the picture changes. Late afternoon cirrus clouds gather into an ensemble of lyres and curlicue harps, a desert-blue shell with gossamer, floating musical instruments. An hour of that, and at our next stop, we're watching sunset, the last molten bead under a line of cirrus clouds blowing upwards like bangs. The land becomes as quiet as a great iron bell not yet struck.

"There she goes," I say.

Irvin says nothing, which is a more appropriate reaction as he points his front tire and starts forward again. This is the simple structure of our day, working out miles, stopping to walk the bikes, and then back on for more miles as the silence opens wider.

Our first tarantula appears ahead of me, walking proud across the dusk-gray road. Irvin's now a quarter mile to my rear, and I stop, let my bike down, and drop to one knee, saying *hello there.* Autumn is when tarantulas are most often seen, when they are out looking for each other to mate for egg-laying and gestation, putting them into winter for hatching and venturing out in the spring.

The sound of Irvin's tires gradually arrives, and he stops, too. "Thin abdomen," he says.

Starving? Thirsty? Going into winter? Red-haired, copper-colored, he—probably he—moves with a grace only a tarantula has, as delicately as fingertips feeling through a bowl of sewing needles. Irvin stands over me to see because I am on the ground a few feet away from the spider, watching its advance. It's hard to call this creature a spider because it looks like something else: a gentle little land octopus dressed in fur. I keep my movements to a minimum, not wanting to hinder his progress to the other side of the road.

"He's looking for a sedentary female," Irvin says. "He's trying to pick up a chemical signal."

When night falls, he'll tuck in somewhere, waiting out the chill, able to see a few inches ahead, no stars in his eyes other than the ambient glow of the sky. As we appreciate his tender progress, the last sun touches each summit above us. The tarantula turns toward me, sensing light, shadow? "Warmth," Irvin says.

With its slow, fluid gait, body suspended as if on a gyroscope, it arrives at my hand on the ground, pausing, feeling. "They need to reach a knuckle or something to bite," he says. "They can't lower their fangs that far." It's the same thing he'd tell kids when we'd find tarantulas in the desert long ago. We'd clear a space, moving back several feet so nobody would involuntarily stomp on it. We'd ask if they wanted to put their hands out and let the arachnid walk over their skin—an activity we were asked by our boss to stop, for some reason. But if the kids were gentle, we'd urge some of the braver or more curious to try it. Put your hand on the ground, lay it flat and directly in the tarantula's path. Put your weight on it so you don't accidentally freak out and throw the fragile animal. Then, feel the tickle of its graze, its slight weight, and the peculiar sensation of an ending when it steps back to the ground.

From leg tip to leg tip, this tarantula is as big around as a coffee mug. It crosses over my thumb and tucks its head and forelegs into the crook of my hand. Tiny eyes glitter above the sheathes of its fangs. It seems comfortable, and I feel chosen. It found its niche, the dark warmth of my cave, possibly a place to wait out the night. I look up at Irvin and say, now what?

We haven't seen much in the way of wildlife. Most flying migrants have gone south by now; we sometimes see a hawk and a few turkey vultures teetering in circles. It's a low-movement time of year. We'll see several more tarantulas before dark, jumping our bikes to miss them.

Where I live, in the high desert in Colorado, the tarantula migration happened about a month ago. Leave the door open, and they'll tap their way in, ending up on the kitchen floor, where you let out a shriek to keep from stepping on one. They are not technically on a migration; they are simply on the move, not going in any one direction but all over. I admire how they follow whatever elements touch their senses: chemical signatures, vibrations, movements in the air, and whatever they see inches ahead. When I lift my hand, I go slow and the tarantula's legs reach out to feel for what's going on. Its body opens as it loses its shelter and begins navigating the road again.

About forty-five miles as the crow flies from the Strip is our first sighting of the North Star. We're camped along the boundary of military land, nested near a low spot between mountains, Joshua trees tipped south toward the sun of winter. We're both hobbling around, groaning like tin men. We lay our gear on the ground as the last fibrous light of day disappears. Bands of color retreat in the west, and Las Vegas rises like the dead from over the horizon. Ten stars become twenty, then thirty. I don't know who first spots Polaris, as small and quiet as a mouse, but soon we're both staring at it, and maps or no maps, we know exactly where we are.

Locating the North Star, Polaris, is an excellent first step in acquainting oneself with the celestial sphere. My method is a glance to the north, picking out the Big Dipper on one side of the sky and then the widow's peak of Cassiopeia on the other, and it's about midway between the two in a somewhat vacant region. There are other ways. Whatever trick you've got, do it habitually and in this hemisphere you can find north without much thought.

Polaris is the principal navigation star, the one that, but for the tiniest wobble, doesn't move in the sky. The full name is Stella Polaris, the Pole Star. It's luck of the draw that we have one, thanks to the Earth's slowly variable axis and thanks to this triple-star system 433 light-years away, their three orbits close enough they look like one. Our wobbling axis brought Polaris into line about 1,500 years ago and will send it off again in another thousand years, back into the nightly flow with the rest of the stars. In 3000 BC, our axis pointed directly toward a white giant hundreds of times more luminous than our sun in orbit with a smaller, dimmer star. Known in Western traditions as Thuban, in the constellation of Draco, this was the pole star of the ancients, and Egyptians took careful note of it when building their pyramids. For a long time, there was nothing between the two stars, and north remained unmarked. Since we're alive in this particular epoch, in the time of soft-spoken Polaris, it's worth knowing how to find it.

I give up counting stars at forty because I can't keep going without losing track. I'd need a box to look through, a frame, something better than holding out the spine of my journal, using it as a straightedge and counting stars along the line. We're seeing a couple hundred at least, with few anywhere near the radiant bulge of Vegas. The rest of the sky is filling nicely. This is a big jump, and I'm finding myself optimistic. The stars are no longer downy little feathers; they've gained sharpness and color. The first satellite I've seen moves across the zenith, a blue zinger. Its wings of solar panels pick up sunlight and bounce it back, making it look like a headlong star. I'd started to miss them. The meter reads 19.96, putting us firmly in Bortle 6.

Green and red are our headlamp colors, and our motions are practiced, the stove pulled out and assembled, water bottles poured carefully, not a drop wasted. It's good to get into a familiar rhythm, our hands moving the same ways each evening. We sit on our little squares of closed-cell foam pads, more comfortable than being on limestone hex nuts scattered across the ground. The earth has coughed itself into little pieces, a few rocks bigger than a knuckle, not comfortable on the rear. Our shadows are still evident from Las Vegas, as bright in the distance as a gibbous moon freshly risen. There is no campfire tonight, just the sky and the gray of Earth.

It's so quiet that every move we make sounds as if we're inside a capsule. There's a difference between sounds up close—putting away the stove, closing up gear—and the sound of faraway, the infinite echo of the heavens. The highway is fifteen miles behind us, far enough we can't hear or see it.

The day was a long push and we don't have much to say in our dark spaces. There was one flat, Irvin's back rear, and we'll fix it in the morning. We are sore, creaky, and quiet. After dinner, Irvin heads for his sleeping bag. I wander through the stillness, filling pages in my notebook from the day, my green light on, reading glasses perched on my nose as I write about reaching our first cache that morning, digging water jugs from an abandoned coyote hole half a mile off the highway, three gallons each because any more than that might crack the hubs on our bikes. This early resupply was a booster, topping us off to get us through a mountain range and across the next basin. Though we'd only buried the cache a few days earlier, it took ten minutes of wandering between paper-seeded frazzles of saltbush to find which abandoned coyote hole we had used. It was a simple cache, only water, and we carried the crushed plastic jugs along with us, making us look like we were on some kind of deflated balloon adventure.

Initially, we planned to make this trip with gravel bikes, which are lighter and leaner in frame. Fortunately, we were talked out of that. The powerline road would have done us in, left us with warped spokes and busted gear. The firefighter we connected with in Vegas, a nephew of a friend, is an avid backcountry biker and he loaned us these two mountain bikes, low-geared grinders with three-inch knobby tires. I'm not much for this sport to begin with. It feels like hyper-speed, an insult to an ambling person's taste, accustomed to putting one foot in front of the next as we humans have done since the beginning. You can moderate your speed on foot, going quietly or walking freely. You can stop and pick something up, scribble a bit in the journal, and have a seat on a boulder. A fully loaded bike is like pedaling a tank that doesn't want to stop. I have to keep my journal strapped to the front in case I get a chance to pause. The firefighter was right that we needed these bikes for our route. He was also right when he said to avoid highways and aim only for dirt roads. This plan put us into deeper country, no powerlines here, just two vehicles passing since we left the highway, both four-by-fours well-dusted and marred by light body damage. One of them slowed, a Ford Bronco with the window rolled down, Nevada plates, the driver asking if we were okay.

At almost eleven at night, I finish the day's notes. Irvin is snoring gently, and my eyes are pretending they can see the Milky Way. It's almost there, a ghost trying to reveal itself. After a few tries, warming up the light meter and pointing it toward the darkest part of the sky, I get a reading of 20.9, almost two points darker than last night. We're crossing a threshold, entering the unbright side of the world. Having stars back is exciting. Vegas light still occupies most of the view with half-formed Pegasus climbing out of the

henshit-colored dome. Jupiter takes on a defined shape, a punc-
tuation mark rather than a speck. The Northern Cross, which sits
in the constellation of Cygnus the Swan, has formed where there
had been random dots of vague stars the night before. An atlas is
forming, the truest map we have.

In the Barrenlands of northwest Canada, the night sky has long
been the primary map used for dogsleds and snow machines on
long crossings. A subsistence dogsledder, Fred Sangris, of the
Yellowknives Dene First Nation, co-authored a paper in the *Journal of the Arctic Institute of North America* where he documented
how to navigate by stars for two or three days along a featureless,
snow-covered route. He said he'd watch for the rising of Arcturus,
which told him when to start and what bearing to take. Once on the
trail with his dog team, he'd watch for the Pleiades cluster rising
into what he called "noon position," and he knew it was time to rest
the dogs and sleep.

Sangris explained,

So, in the Barrenlands it's dangerous kind of to travel
during the daytime, especially if it's whiteout. You have
no idea where you're at. But if the stars come out and the
sky is clear and you're traveling, that's the safest. For me
that's the safest way to travel because I've done it many
times. And then I watch the east sun, or the star from the
east. I would pick that, I would pick that star. There's lots
of stars. Remember, lots of stars in the sky, eh. But I pick
the unusual star and I keep my eye on that star. And I keep
traveling, traveling a great distance. And then it comes
right up like that. Just like that. Just like that, and then
I would find another star over here not too far from that
and I would pick that one. I'll pick on that one for a little

while. I'll keep going, eh. After a while I'll stop and I'll pick up another one here. And that's how I get from one end to the other end.

Following stars is perhaps the simplest form of celestial navigation. It's hopscotch: Mark out a star in your head, and find another that moves into the same position as the starfield progresses. In a big sky, there are plenty to choose from. Keep finding stars that move into the same position, and you'll have an artificially fixed point in the sky.

In the heavy sea trade on the Mediterranean more than two thousand years ago, sailors out of Crete did the same as Fred Sangris. Steering across open waters, they'd start with pivotal stars at the points of rising and setting, and then replace them with whatever came up next along the path. Minoan palaces were oriented toward these lodestars, their throne rooms set to celestial alignments, as if by stepping out to see the sky each night, you could see the wealth of trade pouring in. These were the big-gun stars—Castor, Arcturus, Altair, Spica, Aldebaran, Sirius, Rigel, Betelgeuse, and the phosphorescent triad of Orion's Belt. Each would rise over the position of a trade city out of sight some five hundred miles across the water. In turn, archaeological study of these cities has produced many artifacts from Crete, where one end of a star path materially connected to the other.

This is also what Polynesians famously mastered over millennia of travel and migration across Oceania, crossing thousands of miles of ocean with no land in view. They, too, employed a pattern of stellar replacements. There were other cues to help point the way: Birds and clouds were part of the calculus, and waves lapping against the hull spoke to the direction of the drift, currents affected by landmasses well over the horizon. But without stars, humans would have been directionless on these long journeys, utterly lost.

Different star-following techniques are reported by Gwich'in Indigenous communities in the Alaskan Arctic around the Yukon

River, a thousand miles from Sangris' route. Instead of the classic star-after-star method, Gwich'in open-ground navigation involves a single constellation called Yahdii that takes up most of the sky. This represents a mythic foxlike character comprising sixteen star groupings symbolizing different parts of Yahdii's body. There's a strapped bag on one side, and one hand holds a crookneck staff. The Milky Way is the snow-packed path Yahdii is walking. Because this legendary figure is a single, continuous constellation, a glimpse of its stars even on a cloudy night can be enough to help a traveler reconstruct the sky's map from memory.

I traveled by canoe in the Arctic interior of Alaska, in Gwich'in territory, where the landscape of the Yukon Flats is almost featureless, the horizon a single circle mountainless and darkened by islands of black spruce. Rivers wind around each other in endless oxbows and sloughs as if the landscape was deliberately trying to get a person lost, no highways or roads for hundreds of miles. I was there in summer when the sun looped around our heads without even a hint of night. My companion and I not only lost any sense of space, but we also lost time. The two became so transparent we could not find ourselves in either; morning the same as midday, the same as night. For five weeks in the wilderness, the names of days escaped us, east and west going anywhere they wanted to. Unsure how or when to sleep or wake, my circadian rhythm stuttered, and I felt as if I were sleepwalking or sleep-paddling, as it were. We would pull our canoe into villages, where the locals told us winter is much easier for travel; the rivers freeze, and the land becomes solid. The sky is a map and by the stars of Yahdii, you always know how to go. I'd never been away from the night for so long. Not a star to be seen, the full moon as faint as ash—it felt like another planet, yet it was very much this one.

As we traveled between villages, we heard a familiar language being spoken, closely related to Diné, the Navajo language of the Southwest. This linguistic connection says that at one point, people from the desert and people from the Arctic share direct ancestry.

The Navajo Diné have well-developed star lore that stands out among Indigenous cultures. In sandstone caves in what is now Arizona and New Mexico, they stamped stars on the ceilings of natural stone alcoves using black, white, gray, red, and orange paint. Long ago, these Diné came to the Southwest as nomads from the Far North, carrying a host of legends about how the universe was first organized, how the stars were carefully placed one by one, and how trickster Coyote grew impatient and scattered them everywhere to make a wild mess of the heavens. These legends began far away and traveled, taking root in a land where the people are said to have come out of red desert ground and where they eventually painted stars over their heads as if bringing back the memory of Yahdii.

In my own way, I stumbled on stellar navigation out of necessity. I was with Irvin years ago. He, a third companion, and I crossed a sand field on foot, a few thousand square miles of wind-shaped dunes in the Gran Desierto of Sonora, Mexico. Often, we walked at night to avoid the heat. Stars, we found, were the best way to keep our bearings, the same as Minoans, Polynesians, and Fred Sangris. To use a compass, you'd have to stop and shine a light on it, lining up the arrow and hoping you could hold the heading while moving through dunes sloshing like a tumultuous sea. Stars, on the other hand, are permanent. They are like pegs on a board.

We'd stop with our feet in the sand, heavy water loads on our backs, and confer to ensure we were still on track. As stars emerged over snaking horizons, we would decide which one was next—the lodestar, the one you lock onto.

In the dunes, the three of us often walked into sunrise and continued for a couple more hours. Wind snaked around us, turning the air prismatic with blowing sand. We experienced hallucinations, as we later confessed to each other, owing to those long hours of mindless trudging turning into fanciful waking dreams. One hallucination we all shared. It only happened during the day, flashes of silver that we saw at the edge of our vision, bright enough to make us turn our heads. Morning by morning we wondered about it, and finally figured it out. At night, with our eyes anchored to certain stars, we saw messes of meteorites. Our gazes were focused up, the dunes were black, and the night sky was a spectacle, putting our peripheral vision in high gear. We'd pick out little sparkles I'd never seen before—the Earth passing through clouds of meteors the size of sand grains, the upper atmosphere twinkling with tiny impacts. The bigger ones, long streaks of blue or green or yellow, came from good-sized rocks made of iron or ice burning up on impact, and those would cause us to stop in our tracks and shout in the dark. We saw fewer shooting stars as dusk came on, but the bright ones persisted. The sun would rise, the day begin, and we realized the streaks of light we'd been seeing were meteorites catching the far edges of our vision in broad daylight. The parts of the eye that pick up the most subtle illumination—primarily black and white rods and fewer color-sensitive cones—detected subtleties of light we would usually miss. The result is that we were seeing shooting stars during the day.

Humans aren't the only creatures that look all the way up. If a dung beetle in a contained arena has a white streak painted above it, it will tend to roll its dung ball in line with the streak, following it as if it were the Milky Way. Using their hooked hind legs, dung beetles roll their balls across featureless terrain at night, using the splash of our galactic disk to keep from going in circles.

Yellow underwing moths cue onto the Milky Way precisely where it passes through the constellations of Scorpio and Sagittarius, one of the most star-lit parts of the night sky.

In 1949, German ornithologist Gustav Kramer observed that when birds in cages were left outside on clear nights, they often went to the corner of the cage that corresponded with the direction of their migratory path. The night sky was guiding them. This observation was taken further in the 1960s by Stephen Emlen, a behavioral ecologist at Cornell University specializing in the orientation and navigation of migratory birds. Emlen placed indigo buntings, which are nocturnal migrators, in planetariums during the seasons they'd typically be in motion. He kept them in funnels with mesh tops, leaving enough room to flutter in one direction or another but not to fly away. Ink pads were placed at the bottom of the funnels so that when the buntings landed, their feet picked up some of the ink, and when they took off again, they scrabbled against the sides of the funnel leaving marks that showed their preferred direction. Using these funnels inside of planetariums, Emlen could narrow down what the birds might be using for reference. When he removed the constellations, the buntings in the funnels did not change their directional behavior. He turned off the Milky Way, and there was still no change. Every star but one was taken away, and that was Polaris, the only star that doesn't move, or at least that one that moves so little it's hardly worth mentioning. That was the one, the star the buntings are watching.

Emlen changed the orientation of the sky so that instead of Polaris being at the pole, Betelgeuse became the central star, with all the other stars now revolving around it. The ink from the birds raised under this new alignment showed that they switched to Betelgeuse, and Polaris meant nothing. They were fixed on the pole, whichever star that might be.

When every star was turned off, and the planetarium was softly lit from all around, the ink went everywhere. Birds didn't know where to go.

My sleeping bag is an astronomical observatory. The hood is cinched almost closed, with a circle left above my nose so I can breathe and still see out. Four thirty in the morning, I lie on my side watching Venus, no sign of gloaming, the sun not yet creeping around this side of the planet. The mountains are darker than the sky, and they sit in lotus postures of stillness. I've been awake for at least an hour, unwilling to get out of my bag. If the air had enough moisture to make frost, we'd be caked with it. But there is none.

The chrome sparkle of Venus emerges from the eastern horizon. This is as bright as Venus appears, positioned in what is known as its greatest western elongation, at its farthest from the glare of sunrise. I can see where the Milky Way ought to be, my brain trying hard to put it there, and maybe I do see a tiny bit of it sprinkled at the zenith. The twin stars Castor and Pollux, a pairing I haven't glimpsed till now, are down by my knees.

I roll onto my side to see the false dawn of Vegas, and then my other side for Venus. Irvin is probably awake, memorizing the firmament like me, watching this planetary rising, which is the biggest thing to happen in a couple of hours. Mountain ridges and sharp desert plants rake at the edges of the sky. One prickly Joshua tree stands black-on-white against the city dome.

A down vest is wadded at the bottom of my bag with my socked feet stuffed in it, and everything else that I have I am wearing, or else is tucked in around me, and still, I'm not particularly warm. I am a pair of eyes at the head of a synthetic green caterpillar, stretching and squirming as if trying to grow wings. The day is beginning, the eastern atmosphere touched with fuchsia.

Venus traces a bright fingertip along the ecliptic as if hinting at its departure. Stars close their eyes one by one. Fuchsia is now orange, becoming yellow, and the morning star, as Venus is sometimes called, hangs by a thread. A white vault forms where the sun will rise on a crisp and cloudless morning. At 5 a.m., dawn and city-light are equal. I can't find the sharp white planet anymore, and I'm turned, facing westward where the veil of night slides back, pooling somewhere over the horizon. At 6 a.m., daylight touches the tops of mountains forty miles away. Space is wiped clean, nothing to show for it but our closest star, the brightest by far, the one that says it's time to get up.

BORTLE 5

* * * * * * * * * * *

Only hints of the zodiacal light are seen on the best spring and autumn nights. The Milky Way is very weak or invisible near the horizon and looks rather washed out overhead. Light sources are evident in most if not all directions. Over most or all the sky, clouds are quite noticeably brighter than the sky itself.

* * * * * * * * * * *

BORTLE 5

The house where my children were born had a single switch that turned all electricity off. Before climbing the ladder to the loft for bed, one of us would tap the switch and shut down ghost loads and tiny bricks of diodes that stay on for no good reason. The internet's inaudible purr ceased, and the moon and stars could drift freely through our windows. We were on solar, our winters powered enough to get us through most days, with nights dimmed out of habit, oil lamps set around the house with their small blades of flame. For me, it was a familiar and promising way to live, a home silent at night, wires in the walls no longer hot.

Later, we got indoor plumbing and more solar panels, enough to keep most of the lights on in the gloom of winter. We no longer had to walk outside to the tap for water every night. That was something I came to miss, those times of waiting for buckets to fill, nothing to do but study the night and feel the million tiny needles of the Milky Way land like snowflakes on my cheeks.

What would our lives be like if we could turn everything off occasionally and step outside to look up? This is why urban power outages excite me. Aside from traffic signals being out and hospitals turning on generators while your freezer starts to thaw, there are benefits: We get to see the world as it was, as it still is. Moths resume whatever they were doing; birds correct their flight paths instantly. Even the humans fall silent, the only clatter coming from the frantic hunt for batteries in a kitchen drawer. I was a kid in Phoenix when the power went out city-wide. With the air conditioning off, we opened doors and windows and sat on the roof watching star milk spill onto the roofs around us.

In my twenties, the guiding outfit Irvin and I worked for sent me to Bahía de Los Ángeles on the inner coast of Baja, where my job was to identify kinds of granite and cactus for an Elderhostel trip. This was 1994, and we were three hundred miles from the nearest urban glow; the only electricity in this Mexican fishing village came from diesel generators and solar panels. Outdoor lightbulbs were the old gas discharge variety, naked and dusty under palm-frond palapas. One hung by a pair of wires in front of a whitewashed bodega, luring moths and spiders. The little town didn't touch space, had no effect on it. When stars lowered into the sea one by one, I thought they would hiss.

After the trip, we returned to Southern California, arriving on a date that would prove auspicious: an historic power outage would hit early the next morning, a full-blown coastal blackout. Our time in Bahía de Los Ángeles primed our eyes for the event. In the bigger Los Angeles, showing up late at night, our eyes sizzled in their sockets from orbs of sodium vapor flying past by the thousands. I sat in the passenger seat while another guide drove the company van, hauling a loaded kayak trailer. There was so much brightness, action, and noise we both felt like we were going to be sick. I had a paper map in my lap, but I couldn't tell north from south or one municipality from another. We had a place to stay, someone's apartment in Pasadena, an address scribbled in a notebook, so we pulled over at a gas station to ask directions. My partner went in with the map while I climbed onto the van roof on top of our tied-down cargo heap, hands cupped around my eyes, doing the only thing I knew how to do. The sky looked like the inside of a grapefruit rind. I teased out the bloodspeck of Betelgeuse, shoulder of Orion, and then a couple of the constellation's belt stars. Between what the gas station attendant offered and my being able to tell north from south, we found our way to the friend's place to park the trailer and get some rest.

In the darkest hour before dawn, the Northridge Earthquake struck, throwing me from the couch where I was sleeping. On the third floor of an apartment building, everything lurched violently back and forth—magnitude 6.7, epicenter directly under the city. Overpasses pancaked on top of each other and cars that had been in motion tumbled into fissures. At once, every light went out.

This was a jerking kind of quake that pitches a person across the floor, in my case wearing the bedsheet I'd been sleeping in. The shaking subsided after a solid, terrifying fifteen seconds, and I stood up with my feet braced, heart pounding, in a room so dark I could barely make out the shapes of books and knickknacks on the floor, the lamps that had toppled. After we found each other and put on clothes, we joined the stream of people heading down the stairwell and out into the street amid the howling of sirens and voices murmuring, shouting, a flurry of excited conversations, breathless stories already being told about what had just happened.

Without the constant photon bath, skinny strips of lawn and the leaves of shrubbery relaxed. The entranced eyes of insects snapped out of it. All of us were now awake, staring around as if we'd forgotten where we were.

In the absence of a visible moon, the darkness stretched farther than any of us were aware of, blackouts coursing along a collapsed grid through Nevada, Wyoming, Idaho—all the way up to Alberta. The blast of darkness radiated off the West Coast and took out cities, and the continent's night map changed instantly. Anyone coming out with a flashlight instantly blinded themselves and anyone right around them. Yet our pupils soon widened to take in the unexpected night. With streetlights and checkerboards of windows snuffed out, we could see each other standing along sidewalks and streets, gathering at corners as if by instinct, and the luminance around us came from stars and interplanetary dust. The Big Dipper floated straight overhead like a compass. Calls poured into emergency centers and local observatories claiming that strange lights were in the sky, panic over what was being called "a giant silvery cloud." People were seeing zodiacal light from space for the first time.

I didn't live there or have a stake other than still being alive. The walls that had cracked were not mine. Even if the van and its trailer and kayaks vanished into a hole in the parking lot, I could still walk away. I was allowed to look up with impunity. The plug had been pulled and night returned as bright-eyed and bushy-tailed as ever.

Morning shadows move as slowly as our bikes following this rocky bloodline of a road. We're hardly kicking up dust, our tracks weaving around rocks in the way. The climb is long and slow, a couple of miles per hour, just fast enough that we don't fall over. In four-low washouts, our tires spin, and gravel strikes frames and forks like chimes. Water is a worry. The work is warm, the bands around the insides of our helmets soaked and dripping as the day goes on. When your kidneys are getting hammered with thirst, you realize that having enough water matters. We brought as much as we could, but we still don't have quite what we want. One more quart each, and we'd be set.

Mountains lean back as if looking up, each an observatory. Tectonic actively wrenches apart billion-ton rock blocks while the basins between them spread open, leaving ten- and twenty-mile-wide stretch marks across this restless side of the continent. The Basin and Range Province, a chunk of arid Western landscape from Oregon deep into Mexico, including almost all of Nevada, is a tiered garden of salt flats and dust. Bone-parched basins were left by ice ages when they held fresh water, like great mirrors with riparian shores. The lakes dried and the land cracked. It's not particularly habitable country, not by modern standards. Towns lie thirty miles or a hundred miles apart. In the 1990s, there was only one phone book for the entire state, and I thought it was the finest honor a landmass as large as Nevada could claim. Roughness has kept people out. More to the point, it has kept light out. The landscape is for the most part unplugged.

Behind me, Irvin calls out and I crunch to a slow stop, looking back. He's looking back, too. A rooster tail of dust winds up the road a few miles behind us, a train of five Jeeps banging hard and throwing rocks as they go. I'm thinking about that extra quart, and Irvin is too. People in the Jeeps are probably carrying it.

A wiry, muscular man with a goatee and ball cap, maybe in his forties, rolls down his window on his empty passenger seat as he stops, asking if we're okay. He's got Nevada plates. I say we're great, it's a beautiful day. Irvin concurs, and the driver agrees.

"If we had a couple more quarts of water, we'd be even better," I say. "Would you have any extra?"

"We can do that," the driver says. The other Jeeps are catching up now, and he pulls a CB microphone from above his mirror, the cord extending to his mouth, as he says, "We've got a couple guys up here trekking on bicycles. Is there extra water back there to spare?"

A voice returns, "Affirmative, we've got plenty."

I can't help but smile at that; our day is getting one notch finer. Irvin thanks the man as he comes around, and we shake hands. Leaving his engine running, he asks where on Earth we're going and where we came from. When we say Vegas he laughs because it feels a million miles away from here. They're driving fast because they've got a hundred miles to cover; they hope to be a couple of basins north of here by sundown, camped under a darkness we intend to reach at the end of our bike ride. "That's where we're heading," Irvin says. "Somewhere west of Hiko in four days."

"That's where we'll be tonight," the driver says.

Another man with a larger build in a T-shirt and a jacket comes up, carrying store-bought water. He says we can have whatever we need. "Mind if I down this right here and give you the bottle?" I ask. The head driver says of course, and I see he's missing a front tooth. It's not the kind of thing you mention on first meeting, and I don't say anything, but the young man we met on the powerline road was also missing a front tooth. Water for water. Give some to a stranger, and unexpectedly, some comes back. I'd like to think it works that way. Irvin and I crack lids and empty bottles into our throats in one shot, crushing them and then returning them. More bottles come, and we pour them into bladders and hard-sided bottles we've got hanging all over our bikes.

"These electric?" asks the one who brought the water. The head driver says, "You couldn't get electric bikes this far, not loaded like that." They ask how we like our mode of travel and Irvin says it's easier than carrying a backpack all the time. I say it's nice to have all your stuff packed tight every day, but you never stop pedaling. We know the kind of thing to say in this company, explaining the shocks on the front forks, disc brakes, how the bikes are geared low so you can crawl if you need to, and three-inch-wide tires to get us through the dust. We come away with three bonus quarts of water, and as they drive off, they wave through their windows. We feel like we were handed keys to the kingdom. Crossing the next basin, the largest one yet, will be a snap.

A wilderness once abundant and over all of our heads has been shockingly reduced. Eighty percent of people on Earth can't see the Milky Way. Europe is an eruption on the global night map, as is much of Asia. Outside empires and distant forces fomenting wars for generations have left the African interior mostly blank, but its cities are brighter than ever. Light is historical and political, signs of atrocity in some cases, also signs of expansion and rebound. Around the rim of the African continent, the major cities are the fastest-growing in the world, Africa's population expected to double in the next quarter century, with two-thirds of that boom destined for the bright urban areas. Australia and New Zealand appear to be mostly off-grid while the blaze of Europe reaches across the Atlantic to the colonial fallout of North America, where Irvin and I are in one of the last American bastions.

Darkness is just as historic and political. One reason the West has such clear nights is its abundance of public lands, originally Native lands, taken and held by the US through monstrous bloodshed and extirpation, made into federal property, state property, first by the General Land Office and then by President Theodore Roosevelt who between 1901 and 1909 established approximately 230 million acres of public lands, almost all in the West, including 150 national forests, 5 national parks, 18 national monuments, and 55 federal wildlife refuges and game preserves. Less happens in the human department on these lands compared to east of the Hundredth Meridian with its grids and blocks of private properties. There is no Bortle 1 south of Maine.

We've entered the Desert National Wildlife Refuge, 2,300 square miles of Basin and Range set aside primarily for bighorn sheep, and last night we slept at the edge of mostly empty Nellis Air Force Range and the Nevada Test Site, which covers 5,000 square miles. What this means is a shopping center with a parking lot looped around it and illuminated all night long will not be built, nor will horizons of housing, stadiums, gas stations. The Air Force could go hog wild, but the land will likely remain similar to the neighboring wildlife refuge, even as flyovers roar past.

My family is from southern reaches of the Basin and Range Province, Big Bend country in West Texas and nearby New Mexico. Motes of town lights float in a dark sea, much like they do for the rest of the province from there to Oregon. Back then, Basin and Range was a continuous Bortle 1 more than 2,000 miles end to end with dots of isolated cities for islands. When my parents were kids in the 1950s and 1960s, North America was mostly lit along its nighttime coasts. The spider web of the East Coast reached into the country's interior, while the West Coast blossomed but made little headway across the Sierra Nevada into the interior

West. From space, the whole of the Basin and Range would have appeared lonely, only if dark places are considered forsaken. My mother's birth town of Alpine, Texas—population currently a few hundred more than it had in the 1950s—is surrounded by skies as dark as dark can be. My dad grew up in Roswell, New Mexico, alien country. His town sits off the edge of a Bortle 1 that persists to this day, much smaller than it used to be, hundreds of miles of dark instead of thousands, burned around its edges but still hanging on.

Towns and cities that sit on the edge of darkness are gatekeepers. Half an hour out of Las Vegas is Boulder City, Nevada, where the municipality has applied for status as an international dark sky community. Compared to the wasteland of lumens happening in the next basin over, Boulder City seems flush with stars, Milky Way coming into play, a solid Bortle 5. Darkness is good for tourism; not everybody wants their eyes blasted with neon colors and phosphorescent whites. Almost two million dollars was granted to Boulder City by the US Economic Development Authority to retrofit local lighting with more efficient fixtures, cutting costs and lowering wasted illumination, which helps the area keep its rating. Another piece of night survives.

Light is hungry and has to be told to stop. Human agency is required. Boulder City is an example of how it happens, and protecting darkness in one place automatically protects it in all directions. For eight years, Ashley Pipkin, a biologist and night sky coordinator for the National Park Service, has been taking readings to catalog sky quality in parks across the West. She told me they've got a good foothold, and where parks are threatened, she sees new parking lots and new visitor centers going in, or a nearby city pressing on the view. Her job is to figure out how to best mitigate the impact, working with surrounding communities to find consensus on light use. Living in Boulder City, she's been spearheading local lighting and darkening initiatives and the community has been responsive, Chamber of Commerce pleased as punch that lighting is being toned down at a municipal level, making the place more inviting.

I confided in Pipkin that I'm feeling fatigued by the number of major environmental issues on our plates, and now we've got stars to worry about. "I don't feel that way about the night sky, because it's so fixable," she said. "It's an inspiration, to be able to make a change and fix something and feel a sense of reward from being able to do that. I think it's something really good."

It's no small thing she's trying to fix. Even with Vegas crawling up its rear, Boulder City has a respectable Bortle 5 and 4 sky around the edges, and 3, 2, 1 farther out. The city is buffering Vegas on the front lines. Pipkin, in her thirties, started a larger advocacy group working on lighting across almost all of Nevada and parts of five surrounding states, tying Boulder City into greater regions of darkness. This, in turn, protects skies in parks she works for. She told me this is the most extravagant, most amazing island that we have left in the Lower 48, and in the absence of coordinated efforts, light could spread into it unchecked. The larger advocacy group she started is called Basin and Range Dark Sky Cooperative. As a coordinator, she builds coalitions and works with communities, talking to lighting engineers and people who sell fixtures, connecting them with public utilities, forming a darkness grid. She calls it basic infrastructure work. "How many lumens should we have in our environment?" she asked. "The answer establishes a protocol, and we understand what the environmental needs really are, using the correct amount of light."

Pipkin has colleagues working on similar large-scale conservation efforts around the country, each state having dark places and groups formed to preserve them. An eye needs to be kept on the advance of illumination, the same as you'd want firefighters on a blaze. Light gets out of hand as populations rise and light sources become cheaper and more efficient, and if no one is seeing the big picture you end up wondering, like the guard in Vegas, where our night skies went. Pipkin said, "We looked at satellite data and saw these islands and said these are the kinds of remaining dark places we can protect. We parsed it out and thought about these as the different kinds of bastions of darkness where we can try to put the brakes on. This is how we prevent the same impacts we're seeing on the eastern side of the Hundredth Meridian from creeping onto the western side."

The zone Irvin and I are biking into is part of this Rorschach test of dark islands splotched all over the West. These are distinctly outlined, easy to see on a map, generally places where humans are few. If we paid more attention to them, we might name them like parks, preserving boundaries because they could be so easily destroyed. One blank area outside of Albuquerque is shaped like the Japanese archipelago and reaches from Arizona through New Mexico to Colorado. Two Pan-American islands, mostly in northern Mexico, look like a yin and yang symbol; they should probably have two names, like twins. The Colorado Plateau is mostly covered in night, and a big broken-up chain of darkness runs from Wyoming through Montana into southern Alberta and Saskatchewan. Many smaller Bortle 1 zones are embryonic and staggered across the West while the largest of the remaining "night islands" are in the long folds of the Basin and Range. The island we're entering is seven hundred miles from end to end, perforated in the middle by Reno, Elko, and the I-80 corridor. The northern part is mainly in Oregon, and the southern is here in Nevada, with Las Vegas glowering at its edge. We're heading for the middle, the in-between place, the wilderness of night.

There's a word for feeling the loss of the night sky: *noctalgia*. It means night grief. You would feel noctalgic if you'd seen what was here before, if you got out from under artificial skyglow and realized how much beauty is being struck from the record.

I imagine the East Coast as the birthplace of American noctalgia. Poet Adrienne Rich wrote about seeing the heavens from New York City in the 1960s, and her description from a rooftop on a summer evening shows a night unlike what you'll see there now.

> *the Pleiades broken loose, not seven but thousands*
> *every known constellation flinging out fiery threads*
> *and you could distinguish all*
> *—cobwebs, tendrils, anatomies of stars*
> *coherently hammocked, blueblack avenues between*
> *—you knew your way among them, knew you were part of them*
> *until, neck aching, you sat straight up and saw:*
>
> *It was New York, the dream-site*
> *the lost city the city of dreadful light*

One night in the winter of 1998, a few decades after Rich wrote her poem, I went up to the 106th floor of the North Tower of the World Trade Center. I recall how long the elevator took, rocking as it went, pausing partway to open so we could get out and switch to another elevator for the rest of the ascent. That was the technology of the time, the only way to reach this tremendous, swaying height. I handed my coat to the woman at the coatroom and walked into a bar aptly called Windows on the World.

Nocturnal New York City at the end of the twentieth century raged around me, more light coming from outside the building than from the velvety bar fixtures. I got my drink and walked out of that muted pit, climbing a few short steps to the main floor and its museum of windows where I could tell the tourists from the bar crawlers because tourists, like me, bought drinks because we had to, and then walked to the windows with glasses in hand, not stopping to take a sip, standing there and staring 106 floors straight down. The view went to the tips of my shoes, no visual buffer where glass met the tight-weave carpet, and it felt unnerving, like stepping off the edge.

I stared as if I could not believe what I was seeing, as if the bar crawlers must be blind, talking and laughing the way they did. Could they not see what was happening here at the windows? Their voices drained away as I gazed down on this transparent glass fish of a city, every tiny bone of it wired and glowing. If there was any evidence of outer space—Rich's tendrils and blueback avenues—I couldn't see it.

In the spring of 2024, I returned to a similar pinnacle in the city to see if much had changed in three decades. I rode in a crowded elevator, not rattled or shaken this time, propelled directly to the hundredth floor in fifty-two seconds like being beamed to the roof of the skyscraper. Doors opened and a crowd poured into a high-windowed indoor space, looking onto the electric-white boroughs, buildings faced with lit windows numbering in the tens of millions. A revolving door opened onto a windy outdoor viewing platform, where hundreds of onlookers gawked and posed at angled glass barriers tipping away from the building so that you could lean over the edge more than a thousand feet above the ground. Seeing light all around, I felt as if I'd entered the center of the sun, a very different kind of wilderness than one teeming with stars. The Empire State Building stood proudly with its colored spindle making a bold statement, but it couldn't compete with our height. This was a new level of empire, construction on this skyscraper finished in 2019. The Empire State Building, finished in 1931, emerged from the thrumming city like the tip of an awl from a crystalline sea.

What I saw was a different kind of light than what I saw twenty-six years earlier, which had seemed softer, with more oranges and yellows. I hadn't been paying so much attention at the time that I remember the difference exactly, but in 2024 I saw a much brighter, colder-looking city, pegging the blue-white end of the spectrum.

In 2001, LEDs constituted one percent of lights sold worldwide, rising to forty-seven percent in 2019, then sixty-six percent in 2020. When they came on the market, LEDs were lauded as an environmental savior, cheaper and more efficient than the old gas-discharge variety, promoted as a product we could use to save the planet. It's hard to find bad press about them, but the expected drop in energy use never came. Instead, it increased. These lights, which are electric currents passed through semiconductor material, rather than the old version passing an electric current through sealed gas, are so cheap to buy and operate that we've employed them to overflowing.

Meteorological satellites that have been circling the Earth at low altitude since the 1970s have, among other things, been picking up the presence of artificial light, and they show a steady increase since recording started. In 1992, sensors were strengthened for the US Air Force Defense Meteorological Satellite Program, which can detect radiance one million times dimmer than other ground recording satellites. If there's a candle lit, these Air Force satellites can see it. Besides the genuine creepiness of this—the thought of every flick of every lighter being documented—the data are helpful in revealing growth of human presence, something we rarely notice unless we're trying to find a parking space. Along with basic meteorological data, these satellites decipher the spread of light and impermeable surfaces—roads, buildings, and parking lots—solid hallmarks of human expansion. The maps are useful for understanding where development is going, what to prepare for, and what to mitigate. Given how rapidly we're inflating, a baseline is essential for a scientific species such as ourselves, born of trial and error, acting on what works and what doesn't. With a civilization at this scale, you don't want to be running blind. Some thought needs to go into where we're heading.

Over twelve years, between 1992 and 2013, these Air Force satellites detected a forty percent increase in artificial light worldwide. Some regions spiked by 400 percent. This marks LEDs coming onto the market, and the quality of night paid the price. If satellite data seems dubious, there are other ways of documenting the loss of night. Sightings from 51,351 citizen scientists were gathered between 2011 and 2022, and a sharp decrease in the amount of night sky visibility was observed around the world. Each participant in the study, most from industrialized regions, was given a set of star maps and asked which best matched the view at their location. Over the length of the study, the night sky took a hard hit. On average, if two hundred fifty stars were visible when the study began in 2011, one hundred remained eleven years later.

As recently as 2020, Washington, DC, had not gone fully LED, though neighboring Baltimore had already made the switch. From space, the two cities side by side had the appearance of an off-eyed dog: DC was a honey color, and Baltimore was a magnesium fire. From space, the difference between dimmer old technology and brighter new could not be denied. DC is now switching over and the slogan for this new lighting campaign is "Better Brighter." Irvin has noticed this on the street where his family lives, having to draw blinds they used to leave open, the inside of the house turned into a web of shadows when it used to just be dark.

This is not to say LEDs should be shamed or shunned. They can help us find our way out of this problem. Early decades of widespread use saw a fledgling technology with limited range that was overly bright and bad for the eyes. Decade by decade, LEDs have become more efficient and precise, and the range of temperatures and colors has expanded. If they're used intelligently, they don't have to be everywhere and as bright as possible. Brighter better is an old way of thinking.

When I stood at the head of Manhattan in the spring of '24, I wasn't horrified by what I saw. It was more a sense of awe, my eyes lost in the fluorescing maze. I remember lights being softer decades ago, easier to look at. Now, I felt on my toes, my nerves brought to attention. If I ignored the macular degeneration caused by LEDs, and their disruption of the circadian rhythms in our bodies, I couldn't deny my attraction. I come to this city for a reason, and part of that is how it lights up the night. What has been lost is what Rich saw over the city almost sixty years ago, her nightvault swimming with stars.

On this bike ride I'm ground-truthing, squaring numbers from the SQM against what satellite maps are saying. So far, the two are not the same—in fact, they're actively diverging. From orbit, Las Vegas on lumen-maps appears as an angry, white-headed blister radiating outward into red, then a green zone, followed by yellow and gray, and finally the prize we're seeking—black, the darkest of nights. According to these maps, the basin that stretches ahead of us is firmly in the blue, marked as a Bortle 3. But that's not what we're seeing. Last night, many astronomical features you'd expect were still far from visible. It's an open question whether we could detect the Milky Way. That means tonight we'll be in a Bortle 5, not a 3 as the satellites say. The sky maps aren't quite right.

The basin ahead of us is a memory of a Pleistocene lake and it is filled with sunlight. Getting there is ten miles of swift downhill at a hard rattle. We're losing the elevation we spent two days achieving as our bikes become xylophones from flying rocks, the underside of my pedal banging as if from gunshots. At this speed, on the manic side for both of us, the mountains and snaggletooth ridges are visibly coming apart, stepping out of the way to make room for this showstopper basin ahead. We're entering a mirage of tan sediments evaporated from lakes filled and emptied over hundreds of thousands of years. This is a question we've had from the start: is there a navigable way across this basin?

Halfway down to it, we slow and stop to consider our view. Our bones are jackhammered and shaky, but the repairs on Irvin's back tire are holding. He checks his on-screen map and I pull binoculars to bring distances closer, tracing the road until it dissolves into dust. How far am I looking? Roads are not a metric of anything in these basins; I could be eyeballing five miles or fifteen.

Irvin shrugs, unable to tell via satellite if this road keeps going, which will be a problem if it doesn't. The Jeeps haven't turned around and come back, we would have seen them already. I scan for dust clouds, possibly a sign of vehicles mired and trying to get out. There's nothing ahead, indecipherable miles of a perfectly flat hollow that on my paper map is about thirteen miles end to end.

This could be our telescope tonight; the surface is dry and shiny. We could lay our backs on the Earth's great lens and watch the heavens unfold. They'd never let us do this on a real telescope, like the big ones built in the hyper-dry Atacama Desert of South America, telescopes whose ground-glass optics are engineered to precise smoothness—variations no more than 1/1,000th the width of a human hair on lenses nearly 30 feet across. Imagine the uproar if astronomers found us in our sleeping bags on one of their mirrors. We'll end up somewhere on this surface tonight, with a sky clear enough to show another layer of the Bortle.

If the I-80 corridor across Nevada gets any brighter, which it likely will as both Reno and Elko expand, the largest remaining night field in the West will divide, becoming two. That's how dark places shrink, dissolving around the edges, and from the insides out. At a rising pace, artificial light in North America closes in from both directions, with the East Coast clearly winning. The Great Plains and the Upper Midwest are vibrant tapestries fitting the regularity of their terrain. West of the Hundredth Meridian, mountains and a mostly dry and highly variable climate help keep populations at bay, but cities are growing fast, and the corridors are filling. You'd be a fool to think what happened in the East wouldn't happen here, even in these vast and unlit realms. Increasing human population takes its toll on everything, no way around it.

Down in the bottom of the basin, my tires won't move. I'm too tired to make them. For days, the ground has given off the plain smell of limestone, and now it smells of soda. We've changed geology, stirring up a fine substance of Pleistocene origin, a curry-colored powder as fine as sifted flour. Irvin is a long way off, and somehow he seems to have found hardpack. I don't know where or how he's humming along, and the pedals are working up and down. But then he bogs down and stops, and I see him leaning over his handlebars. We've found a dead end. Once my pedals stop moving, there is no sound. If anything, the sky is making a hollow tone, a single note from a giant, open mouth.

"No good?" I ask across a hundred feet.

"Not really," he shouts back.

This road has turned into many roads, each a convergence of ruts caused by four-by-fours trying to escape ponderous dustbins by digging new ones. I wonder how you'd get a stuck vehicle out of here. Do they slowly sink and disappear? Their tires have chopped through murky, desiccated bottoms of Ice Age lakes, the debris of mammoth dung trampled by ancient horse hooves, ages upon ages captured in layers of sediment. The Jeeps we saw earlier must have come through, but the sediment is soft and would have filled in behind them. Irvin and I converge out of necessity, needing to come up with a plan. He says *how about the playa*, gesturing across the bleak interior of the basin. He's thinking we could cross it and maybe find a road on the other side. We have no idea what this untrammeled surface is like, but the one we're on isn't working.

Angling our tires for the playa, we ride cross-country into a dead zone—no creosote bushes growing in the saline pan, just crusty knots of shadscale and saltbush with parched, winged seeds and woody little trunks rimed in chalk. Then, there are no plants at all, as if life has been exhausted, nothing viable here but microbes under sun-cooked crusts in a state of anhydrobiotic suspension. The surface is hard, smooth as an ice rink, scarcely taking any tracks. It's surprisingly perfect for riding, our tires leaving snake-like marks that will be gone in the next wind. The air that's been verging on hot has eased toward the end of the day, turning into a cool breeze that flows across us.

The miles-wide lens of this basin is utterly featureless, and we sail over it as if lifted. The sun is low, shadows from our bikes and bodies stretching out. I let go of my handlebars and sit up as straight as the mast of a sea-going vessel. With easy strokes on the pedals, my shadow traces over what looks like an elephant's skin, the sun honeyed through a thin band of rainbow-streaked cirrus clouds. Jet trails fan into translucent banners at forty thousand feet. This will be another clear night, and this telescope of a basin will give us full range of sight.

The bikes ride themselves. I feel like I should be twirling a parasol over my shoulder. There's no reason to go one direction or another as we arc across miles of geologic depression. You could spread your arms, no need to hold onto anything. After days of challenging roads, this is the simplest sensation, tires purring on hardpack, the sky drawn tight as a drum. Unlike the view from the top of a skyscraper that gazes across a built environment, I see nothing of human making. On the road behind us, I had mostly looked down, attending strictly to the course ahead, and now I can look anywhere, a relaxed form of paying attention. I don't know what good being out here does me, if I'll live any longer or love any better, but at this moment, I feel fully human in the best possible way.

The last fifteen minutes of sun lands on a remote island of dunes, which we're passing from a couple of miles away, a rare aeolian amoeba nestled in the sidewall of this basin. Shapes of sails billow against a backdrop of charcoal-colored mountains burned down as if left too long in a kiln. This was a shoreline fifteen thousand years ago, the wave-washed edge of a lake in wooded, grassy country where Ice Age artifacts were left by people living on seeds and meat. Irvin and I won't see any of their spear points or flakes. We're moving too swiftly, but if we had a day or two to wander this former beach we'd find flecks of worked stone, a chipped atlatl point, perhaps a broken knife blade. What did those people think of the night sky? Their brains were of similar dimension and capacity as ours; what did they say to each other, in whatever language they used, when they looked up at the sparkle every night? Did someone say isn't it strange there's a whole world we cannot touch? It wasn't long after the Paleolithic that rock imagery began to line up with celestial events. Around the world, we calibrated tombs and megalithic structures with sky patterns, viewing star clusters through portals in pyramids, predicting eclipses. It's a good bet that in the Ice Age, people were already looking sharply upward, aware that the world we knew down here was one thing, and up there was entirely another. A wholly busy space stretched over them, about which little was known because it could not be touched or smelled. The year Irvin and I are out, a slight green comet appeared in the sky, and it was last seen from Earth fifty thousand years ago, a Pleistocene event that Neanderthals would have witnessed, and whoever else thought to notice. With its slender white tail and greenish tip, it would have caught attention, probably entering into conversations as eyes raised to see something different in the sky.

We cruise this ancient lakeshore until a road emerges, leading us back into the scrubby Mojave. In the last light, our gear comes out, buckles and straps undone, and I walk around gingerly because, like Irvin, I'm sore and there's been no time for recovery. My thighs feel like they've been poured into a crucible.

Twilight falls at the same time as Las Vegas rises far away, two pale horizons matching intensities for about fifteen minutes before dusk keeps moving to the other side of the planet, and the false dusk of the city remains. We settle into our patterns, Irvin gathering sticks for a fire as I flick a lighter, starting a blue ring of flame on the stove. Under our green and red lights, pouches are torn open, packets of dehydrated foods assembled, and Irvin pulls out the special ingredient we've been using—a bag of dog treats he picked up while we were shopping. I crumble the crisp flakes into our meal from a package that reads "Salmon Skin Baked Dog Treats." He knew we'd be hungry for salmon skin on chilly nights.

In his early twenties, Irvin worked as a fish-counting biologist for the National Marine Fisheries Service in Alaska's Aleutian Islands, going out for a few days at a time on pollack trawlers and cod draggers. He said the crews weren't happy to see him, they had to pay and feed him, as the government requires biological observers on fishing boats to monitor the catch and determine when to stop pollack or cod season. He knew the general conditions of the industry, what parts of fish get canned, packaged, or frozen, and what gets thrown away. He told me that dog treat salmon skin is just salmon skin, a viable food source that would be otherwise discarded. On trips, he always finds odd ingredients to throw in, hunter-gatherer style. "I knew you wouldn't be opposed," he said.

Irvin and I have walked in wild places and subsisted on whatever we could find, prying up shoreline rocks and collecting worms to cook till crisp, sitting around a fire of driftwood and broken-up boat parts, roasting little crabs and gelatinous creatures. If there'd been reality survival shows back then, we'd have been lead characters, but no one was filming us, no one cared, and we liked it that way. Jackrabbit we found stringy, grasshoppers like crunchy grass. We've tried bugs of many varieties. Once, we found ourselves vomiting days into a desert trek from gorging on too many sweet chuparosa flowers. He says his dietary proclivities stem from his coastal heritage, Asian fishing lineages, his family eating more of an animal than most, unfazed by fish eyes or small bones or eggs. His dad ate a lot of odd foods, and so did Irvin, growing up trying beetles, larval bees, swollen ants, aquatic snails, frogs, and the like. He called it protein from low on the food chain, sustenance for island peasants. He went on to study botany and wildlife, curious about living things. "Everything can be food," he said. "Or at least it can be tasted." No wonder he became an Eagle Scout when he was a teenager. He was fascinated with the natural, biological world. Me, I was born this way. I have no excuse. Kids who followed us on trips in the desert seemed to enjoy being in our groups, like belonging to a band of feral foragers. Our only rule was you had to chew, no swallowing like a pill. If you're going to do it, do it right. Our site boss made us quit encouraging teenagers to eat live beetle grubs because, as he said sternly, it was getting out of hand.

Under a spreading pool of stars, Jupiter peeks over an eastern ridge as we sit with our meals, slurping salmon skin dog treats. The coming chill of evening tingles my nose, my cheeks. Night takes about forty minutes to rise to its peak, dusk turned to gloaming and gloaming into dark. The simplest form of the Milky Way has appeared, a brush of light with a dark fault jagged down its middle. The tide of stars has turned, and there's little sense in trying to count them. Only a few are visible in the sky over Vegas, while the rest of what we can see overflows with a new kind of dark, a luster of blackness rising from the north. For the first time, we can see the smudge of the Andromeda Galaxy, the closest galaxy to us at two and a half million light-years. The tiny dipper of the Pleiades, the Seven Sisters, looks like nest eggs huddled together, five of its seven major stars visible. The Big Dipper's handle is fourteen carat, positioned in the right part of the sky to shine its brightest. I can see Mizar, a lower magnitude star in the dipper's handle, something good eyesight is needed to pick out. Jupiter has a healthy color, white touched with orange, not flickering but sharp and steady. Through binoculars, the gas giant has an ill-defined bump around the middle, possibly the planet's largest moons on its equatorial plane.

The view from National Oceanic and Atmospheric Administration (NOAA) satellites puts our basin at a Bortle 3, but it still isn't that dark. This is the same discrepancy the citizen scientist report found: Skyglow on the ground looks different than light emissions observed by satellites. Bortle 5 is a perfectly sweet night sky, enough stars I can say we've turned the corner. I have nothing against this fine view hanging over us tonight, but the satellite maps can be too generous with their interpretations.

Las Vegas is slowly becoming an afterthought, but it still casts a misty shadow, light enough for me to see its glow on my hands. I take measurements from the middle of the road, away from our fire, now a basket of coals with a few lingering flames. A meteorite burns into a streak and dissolves, a grain of something left from billions of years ago, a crusty bit of comet minding its own business until our planet ran into it at 67,000 miles per hour.

Holding out my little electric box with its double-A battery feels laughable until several successful readings give me a magnitude 20.1—Bortle 5, considered a "Suburban Sky." The device seems to be working, showing a slight bump every night. I walk in big circles without using my light, navigating Mormon tea shrubs and shin-poking shadscale spikes, pausing to verify my readings. Another shooting star streaks past, unrelated to the last, in a different direction, from a different source. A satellite moves robotically from east to west, skating across my view. A second satellite sails in from another direction, pulsing as it spins, catching sunlight on its solar panels and then losing it. Half an hour later, I watch a third satellite and am surprised to find myself happy to see them. I say hello out loud to our representative up there and it waves back with its star-like brilliance.

BORTLE 4

* * * * * * * * * * *

Fairly obvious light-pollution domes are apparent over population centers in several directions. The zodiacal light is clearly evident but doesn't even extend halfway to the zenith at the beginning or end of twilight. The Milky Way well above the horizon is still impressive but lacks all but the most obvious structure. M33 is a difficult averted-vision object and is detectable only when at an altitude higher than 50°. Clouds in the direction of light-pollution sources are illuminated but only slightly so, and are still dark overhead.

* * * * * * * * * * *

BORTLE 4

The sky is a way of understanding our place," said Jim Enote, a Zuni farmer, scientist, and scholar from northern New Mexico. Enote and I talk on occasion about old ways of knowing, his ancestry having been in the same four-cornered desert for a thousand years or more. He told me one cannot be sure what is happening that far away, up in the sky. No one can deny it's big, and despite the information we gather, it remains mostly unknown.

"Those things, those stars, are they people holding a torch somewhere?" Enote asked. "Is it the energy and vibration of somebody far away? Is it sunlight reflecting off of something they're holding? It's hard to say. Obviously, we don't know everything. We can say stars are made of these kinds of gases, these kinds of elements, and they emit this kind of radiation in different light spectrums, giant red suns and black holes and all the rest. I think that's interesting, but there's still at the end of the day a question. There's always, we *think* something....There's always, *but*.... There's always, *it depends*....There's something about the sky that has an infinity of many things we don't know."

Enote has stood in his summer cornfield in New Mexico after a long day of work, leaning on the hoe, and he's stared at the sky taking in every kind of light it puts out. He told me, "It goes from a kind of blue-white sky, and then it turns to magenta, purple, yellow, pink, and then a different kind of blue. It finally goes to black or dark. Then the night colors come."

When you see the night colors, you know you've slipped to the other side of the spectrum. That's where the sky begins to express darkness as a form of light.

Enote's appreciation is tempered by a cultural urge to be wary. "Sometimes we're told not to look at the stars," he said. "They could be people looking back at us."

He has told me that he straddles two worlds, something I've heard from Indigenous scientists who stand with one foot in Tribal custom and the other in a colonizer's discipline. From an astronomical perspective, there's nothing to fear out there but bolide impacts, powerful solar flares, and the off-chance of chest-bursting xenomorphs. We don't know really what we're dealing with up there. It would be absurd and presumptuous to believe we grasp it all, or even a goodly portion.

Enote said, "Sometimes, when I was little, the grownups would tell us to come in when it was getting dark, and the sense I got was not just come in and eat, but it was also come in, you have no business being out in the dark. There are beings out there that live in the dark, and it's their place, it's their time."

The Ethiopian night guard I met back in Vegas had said something similar, naming some of the nighttime entities recognized by Indigenous cultures worldwide. He told me one name in Amharic from his upbringing, but I didn't quite catch it. When I asked what the name meant, he said it translates to "children of the night." He said they come down and play, and you have to be careful around them. "They come from other places," he told me. "They come at night and twinkle around."

Enote told me when he ends up working late in his field, or when he's camping, he pauses to take in the celestial brilliance. He said, "You look up at the sky long enough, you see the blue twinkling, the red twinkling, the green twinkling, the whites and the yellows twinkling. The night sky is actually made up of many colors."

Enote sees practical purposes in studying the heavens, whether for navigation or for exploring cosmology and asking the big questions. "Where do we go when we we've left here?" he asked. "Our bones, our meat, our fats will dissolve and go into the soil and nurture grass and plants and trees, and then other animals eat that, and then we eat them. And then we are what we eat, and what we eat is part of being of this place. Night sky, too, is where else we go besides back into the soil. Our spirit will lift, and there may be people above."

In the morning, as we pack in first light, I stare hard searching for Venus, trying to keep the planet in my sights after the sun rises. It's a game of triangulation, using the horizon and a fix on Venus in the post-sunrise blue. I keep track till about ten minutes after sunup and then I can't find its speck of light anymore, lost like a puzzle piece. I lie with my back on the ground, stretched out on rocks scattered like marbles, and survey the sky, the southeast quarter where Venus was last seen, but the planet won't come back. If I had a crescent moon nearby to use as a reference, that would help, but the morning sky with its egg-drop soup clouds is confusing and the moon won't be up for a few more days. Irvin doesn't ask what I'm doing on the ground. He gives me the space I need, and I give up finding Venus again.

In the dunes of Sonora, we came on a blown-out bowl of sand polished by the wind, a circular basin thirty or forty feet across, and I went for the same position, back to the ground, face to the sky at the bottom of the depression. Wearing sunglasses to keep out the sting of blowing sand, I stared straight up in the middle of the day hoping I might be able to see space, there being the fewest atmospheric particles to look through at the zenith. I used the broad pit as a viewing hole, planting myself at the bottom like the receiving end of a mirrored telescope. Seeing into so fierce a blue I'd almost call it black, I wondered if after a while I was seeing nighttime up there, or it was another hallucination from too much time looking at the same thing. You've heard about being able to see stars from the bottom of a daytime well, which I've also heard is not true. But have you tried it? I can't say I saw stars, but if I worked harder, maybe, if I let my eye settle into the light for days, weeks, the heavens might leak through.

On the road by eight in the morning, I stop now and then on my bike and look back in case I might catch Venus. Daytime feels like you can look up all you want, guilt-free, seeing a blue mirror where space has been capped off. There's no universe to see but that bright, hot star we're swinging around. Earthshine coming back down on us is blue because water molecules in the atmosphere absorb the rest of the colors while blue escapes. Variation comes with clouds, and we've got a theater of a day, sun shining through the tissue of high water vapor with whale-shaped floaters moving past at lower altitudes.

The nameless pass we're approaching is not steep enough to complain about, but I'm working as hard as I can to keep a steady mile per hour, two at a stiff pump. Coming out of the last basin, we're in a landscape of volcanic hills and buttes, eroded little alcoves of eyes staring at us from everywhere. Bays of silky, flat-bottomed clouds have moved in, most of the sky gray with a few blue holes peeking through.

A few minutes before I catch up with Irvin, he reaches a cache we'd left near the road. He's collected grocery store water jugs and cans of beer and is walking toward me. I drop my bike and walk toward him, and where we meet is where we sit. Our table is a grainy, rock-hard volcanic ash where I pop open the first can, what seemed like a good idea when we drove in and planted supplies imagining we'd be toasting this last crossing. Coffee-colored foam fills the ring of my can. It smells like the underside of a hay pile. My mouth wants water. I drink. I'm not much of a beer drinker, but this seems like the right occasion, the kind of thing you'd see in commercials, celebrating on the other side of seventy miles of rock and bare basin.

"You going to open yours?"

Irvin takes a breath. He looks more tired than I feel. We've been trading off. I'll sit on the ground like a ragdoll while he's prancing about. "It's been hard to get food down," he says. He opens his can because he has no choice, takes a few sips, and pours the rest on the ground.

I was hoping for a buzz, but that sensation quickly dissipates as we start ten miles of mostly downhill. On the other side of a bulging, rocky notch, the land transforms into Joshua tree-dotted hills and draws. You might think it's a blessing not to have to pedal uphill, dropping a thousand feet in fifteen minutes, but working the brakes and navigating around rocks requires its own kind of energy and attention. I'm doing my best not to crash like a runaway luggage cart, and yes, maybe I'm buzzed now that I'm thinking of it, which has no bearing on my performance because I must have crashed fifteen times in the last several days with no help from a can of beer. Surfing through a sandpit, my front tire catches a wave, floats, then hits a rock and flies sideways. The mess of me and my belongings hits the ground, journal, pen, and glasses landing in the gravel ahead of me.

Up on one leg, I pull the bike to standing position, grab my stray materials off the ground, seat the journal back underneath a strap, and start moving before Irvin gets too far ahead of me.

A change of scene, we knew this part was coming. Our dirt road improves mile by mile until it passes a cluster of mailboxes and a speed limit sign. Soon, it reaches pavement, leading us out of silence and into the din of a two-lane highway that skirts a wildlife refuge around a chain of lakes. These water bodies look like vital organs laid along a basin not near as dry and uninhabited as the last we crossed. Vehicles move fast on asphalt, sixty or seventy miles per hour. I'm leaning on my handlebars, watching them go, waiting for Irvin to catch up after passing each other back and forth the last ten miles. Each vehicle feels like a two-by-four whacking my head as it flies by. Tomorrow, we'll pick up our next food cache and more water, while the highway growls and screams, a roar or two passing every half a minute. We'd been warned not to go by highway but we wanted to travel what's been dubbed "The Extraterrestrial Highway." With the most alien sightings in Nevada, how could you not?

Camp tonight is a metal fire pit with a picnic table overlooking one of the lakes as highway sounds sizzle behind us. The last light of day hangs in November's half-bare cottonwood trees, remaining leaves golden and holding their final light. Where the leaves have fallen, they've begun to smell like rotting citrus, their sugars gone rancid in the autumn cool. Evening breezes fade, leaves hanging still. A purple sky spreads and the east brings up a few stars. Coots prattle and growl in the reeds around the lake, and a heron squawks. The lake surface softens, going from gray to black. Dusk retreats, leaving only the glow of Vegas seventy-five miles away. Stars whisper on the water. Night has begun.

We're not using headlamps much; there's hardly a need anymore. It's not that our eyesight has improved, simply that we've adjusted to our tasks, lighting the stove, fixing a meal, and opening our sleeping bags. The mind works with an enhanced economy in the dark. I know exactly where I put my knife and spoon.

Irvin starts a fire under a big, dead piece of cottonwood, which emits half flame and half smoke. Our fires of late have produced bone-dry smoke from clean-burning desert wood. Lake smoke is thicker and smells like a smoldering mushroom. In the damp coolness, we can see our breath. That's a first: moisture. By morning, we'll have frost.

Big trucks bellow as they pass over a hill behind us. Irvin's having trouble with the noise, remarking three times how quiet it's been, and how he'd forgotten that the world can be so loud.

The Seven Sisters of the Pleiades are now six, which is about as good as the naked eye will do.

I wave my hand over the ground, and though it's slight, a shadow from Vegas is still visible. I count the number of fingers I'm holding up by their shadows on the ground. The town of Alamo, with a population of around a thousand, radiates a bit of orange in the north, but it's isolated, far-off, a meager dose of light pollution. My meter reads magnitude 21.5, placing it fourth on the Bortle scale, identified as "Semi-Suburban to Brighter Rural," actually a damn good sky. The Milky Way looks like itself, with edges becoming cloud-like, as darkness shows down its middle—fields of interstellar gas that absorb light rather than radiate it. I count four shooting stars in an hour. Staying up that evening, kicking around the fire, we probably miss a few. Satellites are numerous enough to be a distraction, flying this way and that.

We're seeing what we used to show the groups we took out in the desert, pointing out Pegasus or Aries, listening for a kid or two to say *holy shit* or just gasp. Our job back then was to get them to look up at least once in their lives and see outer space with their own eyes. I can't say what good it ever did them, who might remember the name of a constellation, or what it felt like to lean back and see a thousand stars at once. Having seen a sumptuous night sky might not be much assistance with the everyday tasks of a life, getting through a job or raising a family in a small apartment, but who knows what could get them through.

The way down to the lake's edge is well-trodden but dark enough to navigate without a headlamp. I go alone, moving slowly, testing ground with my shoe as I reach the water. Reeds and cattails over my head part and the ground becomes soft. At the lake edge I peer out at stars fuller than they were the night before, with the cotton ball that is Andromeda hard to miss. Not a breeze touches the surface of the lake. Jupiter shows itself above and below. There are two Big Dippers, two winged horses, and the Milky Way dips below me and loops back up like a Möbius strip.

The stars Irvin and I are entering have taken on personality, and they don't appear indifferent to me, as they're often said to be. Unaware possibly, but not indifferent, not unconcerned. They aren't intellectually dead the way I've heard some say God is.

Beaming overhead, they live their lives regardless of how we see them, and for all I've heard that stars don't care, I disagree. I just don't know what they care about.

Astronauts have reported not seeing stars from the moon's surface; their footage shows a blank field behind them. This is because being on the surface of the daytime side of the moon is like standing on the face of a spotlight. With no atmosphere to scatter sunlight, it comes down in buckets and the contrasts are too sharp: shadows black, ground white, way more illuminated than Las Vegas Boulevard, Bortle 10 if such a level existed. The moon's dark side, however, holds an entirely different sky, deeper than anything we see from Earth, the negative side of Bortle 1. We have an atmosphere to look through and natural airglow where sunlight wraps around the planet, bounced around between floating particles. Our sky will never be dark. From the shadow side of the moon, there is no light pollution. All you see is space.

An astronaut on the International Space Station filmed the Milky Way from within Earth's shadow, free of any atmosphere, and the stars appear impossibly bright and numerous, as if the station were swimming in sugar crystals. The stars don't twinkle in space, they beam steady. That's why some of the highest-resolution telescopes are in orbit outside our atmosphere. Think of Galileo in his bell tower in Venice, sketching what he saw on the moon through a rudimentary telescope, realizing he was drawing steep, jagged mountains. He was among the first to see terrain, realizing the moon is a big rock. He could see this because he got his telescope as high as he could, above tallow lanterns hung in the streets.

For people I know who have telescopes, instead of higher, they go farther, setting up away from lights, getting out of cities. I have friends I visit, asking if we can open the dome on their little observatory in the backyard where they live on a rural road, or drive with them out of town with equipment in the back seat. I've made a hobby of this. Each year I've got a different object in mind, and lately it's been the Orion Nebula, which I'm thrilled to watch blossom with magnification. This astronomical object is also called Messier 42, a dense star-and-gas cluster in Orion's Belt, visible with the naked eye, making a telescopic view all the more thrilling. My wife and I stopped by the house of a couple we know who live in a dark sky community in the red-rock desert of Utah. They have an observatory out back, and on a clear night—half of a moon seeming to increase the cold winter ground—the wife took us to her husband's observatory. He'd had a stroke a couple of years back, and she'd brought him home to Salt Lake City. From his wheelchair miles away, he directed the observatory remotely and I asked that night if he could connect us with M42.

Wearing coats and warm hats, we walked to the silver-capped observatory out back. She unlocked the door, revealing a hive of machinery and counterbalances attached to the white barrel of a telescope with a five-and-a-half-inch aperture and a camera where the eyepiece would be. The cylinder pointed up at a closed aluminum shell we could see when she turned on a couple of red lightbulbs. The door shut behind us, and it felt like we were standing in a cold closet, a meat locker, our breath curling around us. The woman got on the phone with her husband and went through the sequence. The computer monitor came on, and parts of external machinery attached to the telescope began to whir and click. The device came to life.

The amateur astronomer's name is Mark Bailey. I follow his astrophotography posts online, which showcase lesser-known objects, star clusters with names like Broken Heart, Inchworm, and Spider-and-the-Fly. This makes up most of what we see as background on the clearest nights, a veneer of objects the eye can't quite pick out individually but whose light adds up.

The call went back and forth for several minutes as we watched his shaky cursor find buttons on the screen. I wasn't sure what was more impressive, the man in a wheelchair two hundred miles away operating a telescope that continued to adjust and gyre, or the fact that we were inside a space eye about to open.

Bailey, who works in publishing, inherited the telescope and observatory from his father. He takes pictures of space as a hobby and some of his prints hang in the house—crab-shaped gas clouds in plush colors that his wife and I studied together. He has a black-and-white image of a pillaring gas cloud called the Elephant's Trunk Nebula, and we decide it resembles a woman wearing a shawl over her head standing twenty light-years tall. She's walking through a fog of stars scattering in her wake.

The entire dome rotated, and whatever we were saying to each other stopped. In a robotic motion, the telescope turned upward as the observatory doors shuddered and parted. Moonlight spilled in. We laughed and clapped like children.

"It's working?" Bailey said.

Yes, the space portal has opened! We were out of the closet and into the cosmos with fresh air, stars, and moonlight. One should never be so trapped. Wires and cables ran to the camera like the tentacles of a sci-fi brain linked to the viewing end of the telescope, and the shutter clicked on, staying open for half a minute while we held our breath, and then it closed. The telescope adjusted a notch, and the camera went into action again, layering light over light to distinguish what the human eye cannot.

Bailey often trained his equipment on this nebula, this hazy jewel in Orion's sword, an easy one with quick reward. Images he'd gotten in the past of M42 show a ball gown twirling, folds of fabric wrapped in swirling colors of hot and cooler gases. Molecule factory, star former, it's one of the brighter naked-eye lint balls we can see.

The James Webb Space Telescope, in orbit around the sun a million miles from here, has sent back images of a voluptuous, goat-horned interior, passageways light-years wide sending out new stars like seeds. The Mayans two thousand years ago named this nebula the Fire of Creation. Seeing it clearly with the unaided eye, they knew it was something special, a source of cosmic conception.

A screen of black-and-white static came across the monitor from Bailey's telescope. He mentioned he usually doesn't shoot when the moon is up—astrophotographers seldom do much this time of the month—but he said we might as well see what we can get. With the shutter closed, the telescope moved slightly forward, and a slide was added to the screen, concentrating light into an image. The telescope did what it was supposed to: remove layers of invisibility to peer beyond the atmosphere. Slide after slide resolved into stars filling the monitor, and a phantom of the Orion Nebula began to show—a transparent fetus curled up in the womb of our galaxy.

One of the first photographs of this nebula ever published was from 1883, taken through an 18-inch refractor telescope stuck out of the back of a London garden shed. The image, which won the Royal Astronomical Society's Gold Medal for the year, was taken by Andrew Ainslie Common, an English amateur astronomer, and it shows a nebula unfolded like a dark hand holding a burning lotus. It was the first long exposure revealing much more detail than the eye could get through a telescope of any distant object. Using a camera allowed more light to collect. At the time, light-years were already a form of measurement, giving this photograph not a nearby sense of scale like the moon or Mars, but an unfathomable size, a sprawl of gasses and stars light-years across.

I went to the telescope and followed its focus through the open doors to Orion sprawled sideways across the edge of a Milky Way nearly burned out by the moon. I could see no evidence of the fuzzy nebula hanging in Orion's scabbard, hardly a sign of the scabbard itself, with the moon as bright as it was. I looked back at the screen and saw a hundred times the stars, not necessarily sharp, but definitely visible. The nebula in the middle had assumed the shape of a bat in flight. It lacked any fine details or structures, nothing like what Webb was sending back, but it was there in real time—a stellar nursery 1,500 light-years away, poised in a galactic arm like a permanent firework.

Bailey asked over the phone if we could see it, and we said we could. There was no color on the screen, no sign of an octopus shape you'd get without the moon. It was an indistinct anvil. Still, it was enough to see something enormous and shapely. From a tiny smear of light came a sense of being part of a farther, stellar geography. We were seeing one blossom in an immeasurable garden.

Nobody knows the first time it happened, when involuntary silence fell over a person, or primate, or light-sensitive protozoa looking up at the night. I find it unlikely our species was first. Tonight, wide-eyed tarsiers will be sitting in their jungle trees surrounded by the clicking and buzzing of insects, starlight landing on their moist eyeballs, one of many little beasts looking up, wondering, in various ways, *what is all that*? Harbor seals floating in planetariums can pick out certain stars for reward. I don't know if birds consider what is beaming through their soft bones as they fly into the night, but I suspect ravens and crows have a few thoughts on the matter, gathered on branches at night, eyes wide and watchful.

For humans, the sky first makes a big show in the archaeological record during the Neolithic, along with the first signs of agriculture and domestic animals, tools chipped out of stone and bone, masonry villages constructed around ceremonial chambers. This is where solstice light casts down stone channels and falls on special niches. Spirals pecked into rock are lined up with patterns of the sun, moon, solstice, equinox. This is a Jungian dream, a stage in cultural development when we first proved to the sky that we were looking at it, making tangible, mythic contact between the bedrock here and the expansive there. This is when Stonehenge went up, when vaults and tombs aligned with the heavens.

Archaeoastronomy is a worldwide phenomenon, recording burials and giant earthwork intaglios that were laid out in celestial accord. The pyramids at Giza fall into this category. Precisely aligned with cardinal directions, the largest of the pyramids has "star shafts" running through its interior, each from the central King's Chamber aiming out to areas of sky that were significant during the pyramid's construction five thousand years ago. One shaft had been aimed at the transit of Thuban—the North Star of its time—and another at the position of Orion's Belt as it passed by. Gazing hundreds of feet out through these shafts would have been like standing at the bottom of a well seeing a tiny square of sky, connecting the dead in their tombs to key astronomical bearings.

The three principal Giza pyramids, seen from above, seem to mirror the three-star asterism of Orion's Belt, each pyramid built in the position of one of the three belt stars. It looks like a map, an intentional call-and-response with the night sky. This theory is considered fringe among conventional Egyptologists who point out that the three pyramids are kinked to the north. In contrast, the line of Orion's Belt in the sky is deformed to the south, and the smallest of the three pyramids lies a few hundred feet off from a perfect alignment. Hence, the deformation isn't accurate to the nth degree, which would be odd considering the exacting geodesy of the engineers. The two main pyramids remain the most precisely aligned massive structures ever built, so if the ancient Egyptians could be so precise at such scale, why *weren't* they when they put in the third pyramid, ever so slightly missing the mark? These arguments against an intentional alignment seem weak. Given ancient Egyptian proclivities for sun and moon and all things celestial, an intentional stellar alignment makes sense on a monumental scale, and who knows what to make of this slight inaccuracy? Though they may not have traveled to the stars, they found them to be of great consequence, and these pyramids suggest they may have replicated them here on Earth.

Equinoxes and solstices in the Indigenous Southwest of North

America bring on parades of rock art alignments connecting down here to up there. Sun daggers and bolts of sunrise split circles and spirals at auspicious times of the year all along canyons and cliffs. Sharply pointed shadows land on pecked or painted faces. One center of this activity is the Chacoan system with its extensive ceremonial buildings arranged along a broad, dusty canyon in northern New Mexico. Ancestral complexes stand around like great ant hills with masonry walls rising from the rubble. These tenth-century stone structures have hundreds of rooms built into circles and squares that would be more accurately called temples and not dwellings, many showing scarce signs of being lived in. When the lines of primary exterior and interior walls are extended outward, they connect with celestial features, turning the buildings into time-keeping devices of a sort. The largest of these great houses—a few stories of stonework with a two-acre footprint—is aligned with the solar calendar, while a slightly smaller great house a short walk away is aligned with the lunar calendar. One is the sun and the other the moon.

I've spent long days at Chaco, walking through its toppled floorplans, sitting for sunrise at different times of the year to see how natural light plays with the architecture. In the desert around the canyon, I've camped with great houses breaking the horizon, mounds of ruined observatories joined by thousand-year-old causeways cut and filled into the earth. I've laid myself along these passages wondering what people saw up there. In the desert, you can't help staring at the sky. Elsewhere I'm sure that's true, but here the view is so clear and expansive you can't help lifting your gaze.

Spend a night under the stars, you'll feel a prickle of what it must have been like in Neolithic times. People lived beneath the heavens, knowing phases of the moon and solar positions by heart. The first monumental thing you do as a culture is align your world with the sky. This is the way of ancient stargazers.

A visual artist named Anna Sofaer was part of a documentation crew in Chaco in the 1970s when she came upon a Rosetta Stone of celestial Southwestern rock art. Sofaer worked at Fajada Butte, a castle-headed landform in Chaco Canyon where petroglyphs appear on boulders and rock faces. In profile, the butte resembles a great, stony observatory. Sofaer, in her late thirties at the time, was intrigued by this boulder-skirted landmark. As she ascended the butte on a clear summer day, she sketched and photographed many images on the cliffs, and when she reached the top she came upon a large spiral petroglyph just as a dagger of light was bisecting it. She knew the timing of her encounter with this light event was near noon and close to the day of summer solstice, so she thought it must have been intended to mark this powerful time of the sun's yearly cycle, at its highest passage in the day and the year.

"I was there with no intention," she told me decades later. "I had no theory about what Chaco was, or what the archaeology was about, or who the descendant people were. I was a total innocent, I guess. But what I did have as an artist was a great interest in the works of ancient people, any kind of ritual site, architecture, or monument that related the Earth and the sky. I had studied Mayan astronomy and visited several temples and shrines with research papers proposing astronomical alignments."

The spiral was pecked in the cliff behind three large rock slabs. Returning to the site to record other times in the solar cycle, Sofaer with her colleagues—astronomers, archaeologists and geologists—learned that the openings between the slabs form light patterns that also mark the winter solstice and equinox.

The year before volunteering at Chaco, Sofaer had created photo montages with images she had recorded of five-thousand-year-old spirals etched on boulders at Newgrange in Ireland, and she was reminded of them when she saw the Fajada Butte site. At the time, spirals were appearing in her art work in her New York studio as she explored ancient ways of seeing. Three months before she went to Chaco, she visited the Mayan temple of Chichén Itzá in the Yucatan of Mexico. It was the spring equinox, and she watched a biannual cosmic event at the Great Pyramid of El Castillo where a diamond-back serpent's shadow climbs the pyramid steps at sunset. By the time she got to New Mexico, she was predisposed to sun daggers and lunar crosscuts. She understood that being human has for a long time involved a deep a relationship with the sky and she looked for places where we've connected in the past.

At the time of her findings at Fajada Butte, Sofaer was in contact with Alfonso Ortiz, an anthropologist and member of the Ohkay Owingeh Pueblo a hundred miles east of Chaco, and she showed him photographs of these solar alignments. Ortiz told her, "Where the sun is so marked, so would be the moon." His words ring in her head to this day because she found he was right. Their further study revealed that the eighteen- to nineteen-year cycle of the moon is marked with a pattern of night shadows crossing the spiral. Learning of this complex set of markings and with deeper study of the geologic origin of the rock slabs, she and her colleagues concluded that the slabs had been arranged and shaped by hand, letting through sun and moonlight so that the spiral on the rock recorded the cycles of both heavenly bodies.

Because Sofaer was an artist and not a scientist, and because she was a woman in the 1970s—and also because archaeoastronomy in the Southwest was not much of a thing at the time—her findings had trouble taking hold. She faced pushback from academics, but year after year her finds became more undeniable, and soon similar astronomical features were being documented at many other sites. Some archaeologists say it's too much, that not everything has an intentional celestial alignment. They're probably right, but no one can now deny that early Indigenous civilization in the Southwest was bound to the heavens. If not building temples *to* the sky, they were at least building them *of* the sky.

Phillip Tuwaletstiwa, a member of the Hopi Tribe, has spent considerable time at sites of rock imagery, visiting the remains of great houses erected by his own ancestors. In his early 80s, Tuwa-letstiwa is a geodetic scientist—geodetic meaning the measurement of the Earth's geometry and its orientation in space. With degrees from Ohio State and Cornell University, he has worked as deputy director of the National Geodetic Survey at NOAA and was a longtime member of the American Indian Science and Engineering Society. In the early 1980s, he heard Sofaer give a talk on her findings at Chaco and he was fascinated by the idea that his people a thousand years ago had aligned themselves directly with the sky in ways not so different from his own geodetic survey work. He joined Sofaer's crew of researchers and, with his surveying skills, plotted the orientation of great houses, finding Sofaer was right about their correspondence with either solar or lunar positions.

I asked Tuwaletstiwa what he thought of ancient Chacoan involvement with the visible universe and he responded by speaking about Hopi observance, explaining that the world is divided into three parts: underworld, Earth, and sky. Or Lower World, Middle World, and Upper World. Chopping the air with his hand to show the three levels, he said, "Clearly the astronomical aspects of Chaco and their relationship to the sky are here in the upper world. And we live and farm and exist in the middle world."

The lower world is where people came from, not as commonplace as the sky and the ground, sometimes you forget it's down there. He told me there is a dependence between these three levels, that the middle needs the above and below. "The tree can't exist without the underworld," he said. "It's where it gets nutrients. The tree can't exist without the sunshine and the moisture coming from the upper world."

The tree is us, he said, the living, the mortal, plants and animals and people. We all need both the above and the below.

It's hard for me to tell if this a cultural truth, or just a truth in general, the Holy Trinity, the natural division of the universe as we see it, the sky being one of the three worlds.

"There is also a duality," Tuwaletstiwa said. "Sun and moon, dark and light, day and night. Almost everything has a counterpart. At Hopi you have the katsinas performing their very sacred dances and ceremony. And then, usually around noon, in come the clowns. And they can be what is called Ka-Hopi, which means not Hopi. And they're in direct contrast to the katsinas. Sometimes they do skits or shows and they exhibit the worst possible behavior."

Up and down, Earth and sky, these are fundamental dualities, universal and Hopi at once. The clowns Tuwaletstiwa talked about also come out at nearby Zuni dances in New Mexico, bare-bellied and painted head to toe in black and white stripes, eating slices of watermelon and throwing dirt clods. I've heard of a Zuni dance in the 1960s, around the time of the first lunar landing, when clowns came out dressed like astronauts and hopped about as if in low gravity. That's what the old Pueblo duality thought of the first moon mission, a bunch of clowns doing something ridiculous or even harmful. Should anyone be allowed to touch these sacred bodies in space?

Tuwaletstiwa said the Hopi world is further divided by the passage of time marked in the sky. A timepiece is needed to hold it all together. "On winter solstice," Tuwaletstiwa said, "in the past, before December 21, there was a major ceremony called the men's initiation ceremony. It hasn't been performed for a number of years now, but in any case, a major ceremony, and there was a time they called the dead-time or the quiet-time, leading up to the actual solstice event. That was the time when your crops were in, people could rest, you couldn't work outside so easily. So you would refrain from doing certain things such as digging or disturbing the earth. It was a time for storytelling. And then you come to the Soyal ceremony for the winter. In earlier times, there was always the concern that the sun was in its winter house, and it might stay there. If it did not come out to continue its journey, we would have perpetual winter. So winter is a time for reverence. Long ago, it could have been a time of anxiety or apprehension. And then you restart, you regenerate. You think about planting. You believe the life cycle will continue."

The sky with its many points of traveling light are what assure us of what comes next. We all came out of Neolithic times one way or another, and we still feel the awareness of seasons, Halloween, Easter, school starting, summer vacation. Cycles like this have been running through our blood throughout history. Light comes through windows in patterns you've come to know, a triangle of daylight on a corner of a rug, a square moving across a wall. You might know where to stand at which time in the early fall to see Sirius rise for the first time. It is all patterned and spinning. Tuwaletstiwa said the sky and what happens in it is sacred for Hopi. The moon, sun, and stars are deities, supernatural beings.

"And there's a greater mystery beyond them that sets things in motion," he said.

On his fourth and final voyage to the Americas, Christopher Columbus landed in what is now Jamaica where he intimidated Arawak-speaking people by foretelling the March 1504 total lunar eclipse, which he had gleaned from an astronomical almanac. The people thought he was a god who could control the cosmos, or that's how history tells it. I suspect there must have been a lot of eye-rolling. Who wouldn't have been watching the moon, knowing exactly when and where it would pass across the sun?

Predicting eclipses between the sun and the moon was a specialty of ancient sky watchers, mastered by Greeks, Incans, Mayans. When you start looking up, you start seeing the calculus of the universe. Ptolemy would have told you so. The daytime appears with its crude solar movements, while night tells you everything else you need to know. During the day you can lose the moon, but at night you're aware of its presence when it's up, bright in the sky. This, I believe, is how we began to tell time, seeing heavenly evidence of one season becoming another, old constellations rotating out while new ones come in. Once you get an eye for nighttime, it travels with you all the time.

My last big eclipse was exactly a month before our bike trek, the previous new moon. With two others, I camped for four nights in the Utah desert so we would be adequately prepared for a totality that would last about ten minutes. The center of the eclipse passed directly over the Four Corners, October of 2023, not a solar eclipse where stars become visible during the day, but an annular one where the moon appears slightly smaller than the disk of the sun, which at the moment of totality turns into a blazing ring as thin as floss. We drove a highway south out of Moab, rolling through domes of sandstone, with signs flashing warnings about "Ring of Fire" eclipse traffic along the way. People were into this event. I heard that some of the popular butte-tops looked like mosh pits. Dirt roads took our truck rattling into the backcountry, and when we ran out of road, we continued on foot for a few miles to set camp along sandstone rims the color of raw linen. A natural platform at the end of a long bedrock finger would be our observatory.

If you don't have the time, which I don't seem to have for most eclipses, seeing the height of the action can take an hour or less, but for this one we settled in for the long haul. Camped on bare rock, sitting up in a sleeping bag each morning, one doesn't need an almanac to see what's coming. If you watched the moon reposition itself from one day to the next, taking bearings off the nearby morning marker of Venus, you could see when and where the meeting would happen.

Across a deep gorge to the south, we were within view of the mittened buttes of Monument Valley, markers of the Navajo Nation in Arizona where there's a powerful interdiction around eclipses. It is improper and unhealthy to find oneself out in their strange light. Window shades and curtains are to be drawn. My friends and I were of contrasting ilk, playing with our shadows when the crossing began, casting sickles from between our fingers until sickles became circles as moon and sun entered each other. Horizons around us turned gray at totality, like the surface of another planet, the veil of air not like a total eclipse, more like iridescent silk, an attenuated light held in suspension. A fresh bite of autumn replaced what had been a warming October morning. A drop in ozone and trace gases might have been what I could smell, or it was my brain convincing itself that if everything was changing this much, each sense should be able to detect it.

We watched with special glasses as light connected all the way around the empty circle of the moon, forming a luminous annular ring. Two simple circles moving across a flat sky became dimensional in my eye, turned into two giant bodies in space.

In Diné tradition, seeing an eclipse is thought of like opening a door on an act of love-making, spying the sun and the moon as they go hip to hip. It's not considered something one should gawk at, clapping and waving like we were. The sun is said to die, then come back to life, which is what it looks like, what you start to imagine as you feel the sudden chill and realize how needed our particular star is.

On that day, the Navajo Nation was all but shut down. Tribal parks like Monument Valley were closed, nobody out walking or hitching a ride. Highway stands usually busy with vendors were vacant. Diné commenters online asked folks to please put trigger warnings on eclipse pictures. The aversion is not a monolithic Indigenous belief. Phillip Tuwaletstiwa from Hopi, which sits with its own bloodlines and languages in the middle of the Navajo Reservation, had no trouble watching the event; nothing in his upbringing told him not to. Another eclipse came months later, and Jim Enote from Zuni watched it from the bottom of the Grand Canyon, noting how sixteen condors took to the air at the peak, and all flew the same direction.

The Department of Diné Education posted a statement clarifying the need for discretion:

…out of respect, all activity stops during the eclipse. It's our way to respect the Holy People during the eclipse, along with the atmosphere and the cosmic order. We need to respect the cycle of nature and our atmosphere, and continue to educate younger generations as to why we do so.

According to our Diné cultural beliefs, viewing the eclipse can result in health and spiritual problems. We are instructed not to eat, sleep, or to be out in the sunlight while a solar eclipse is happening. Eating during the eclipse can cause eating disorders, sleeping during the eclipse will create sleep deprivation and watching the eclipse will create eye problems. We are to remain reverent and discourage any activities during the solar eclipse.

It is part of our culture to respect the cycle of life, the path of the sun, as it is the source of all life. As we go through changes in our life, we set a time for ourselves, for self-reflection, a time of peace, uninterrupted tranquility, and reverence, and to show our respect to the sun and the moon.

This is a good teaching lesson for children. We encourage our Diné schools and communities to continue teaching our students about the significance of these beliefs.

To me, this is evidence of how movements in the sky are considered as important if not more than movements here on Earth. Up there is not a thing to be trifled with. It has its own power, which we quickly forget, so busy with our hands and our many tasks down here. Two months after the October eclipse, an uncrewed lunar lander took off from US soil with the purpose of, among many things, robotically depositing ashes from seventy people and one dog on the surface of the moon. The Navajo Nation formally opposed the launch on behalf of itself and other tribes, and took its plea to the White House, saying that ashes of the dead placed on such a sacred entity is a desecration, and sovereign nations must have a say over what we do to celestial objects. Having just witnessed the eclipse, I could see the reasoning. The players are real. The Earth, moon, and sun are not ideas, but bodies engaged in a very large conversation. Again, you don't trifle with them.

Deemed private, not entirely under government auspices, the lunar mission went ahead regardless of Tribal concerns. The ashes were paid for, sent by companies trying moon burials as a new enterprise. Shortly after takeoff, the probe developed a fatal fuel leak and lost its propellant for any kind of soft landing. The mission was called a loss, diverted so it wouldn't crash and leave wreckage on the moon. For ten and a half days before its return to Earth, the vehicle sped through space, sailing in useless silence beyond the orbit of our nickel-and-dust moon with its mountains and enormous cratered basins, before curving back for home. For the cremated remains from seventy people and their faithful dog, the cherry on top was reentry. As it struck the Earth's atmosphere, the lander vaporized like a firework.

On the new moon night of November, I'm walking the edge of a lake with a green headlamp in my fist, fingers letting through enough light to keep me from stepping in water. With the moon between us and the sun, it is essentially gone, unseen, taken wholly out of the sky. This is how we get our darkest nights. Wet ground in and out of reeds is pronged with the tracks of great blue herons. I aim for a spit that reaches into the lake, a black neck stretching beneath a sky more than half-bright with stars. Orion poses on its side, and below the belt is the tiniest ghost of a nebula, the Mayan Fire of Creation

Zodiacal light has begun, the first night I see this oceanic incandescence. This kind of light is from a diffuse cloud of dust particles flattened into a disk around the sun and all the planets. Primarily it consists of comet powder augmented with dust swept off the deserted face of Mars. Particles are rarely larger than dust motes; most are much smaller, the size of bacteria. Spread over trillions of miles in all directions—if that measurement even applies—they account for enough material to reflect muted sunlight back at us, forming coloration among the stars, a band that follows the plane of the solar system across the sky. It's often seen as a cone pointing upward from the horizon before dawn or after dusk. Tonight, it appears as a pallid wisp where the sun was a few hours ago. I'm also picking up reflected airglow from sunlight that fits around our atmosphere like a glove. Put together, these natural sources of space light still aren't as bright as the mound of Vegas on the southern Horizon. There's still a shadow if you stop long enough to see.

The air is riparian, damp on the rings of my nostrils, and it brings out a smell of leaves and mud. Cattail blades brush past until I reach a barren, rocky spit and walk over chunky lake rocks pushed into place by bulldozers. The lake surrounds me. I am teetering over a reflected abyss. Measurements from the meter give a magnitude of 21.5, right on schedule, one more step into this dark island.

Tonight's sky is notably more abundant than the last. Is that Saturn in the west? It is yellowish and not twinkling as much as the stars. Uranus is up, but I won't be able to find it, being one of the lesser-seen planets, easily mistaken for hundreds of other minor points of light. Past the small fluff of Andromeda is the Pinwheel Galaxy, the second-closest galaxy to us at about twenty million light-years away. It's scarcely there with binoculars. With high-powered telescopes, its spiral arms appear tangled with star-forming nebula, like rose blossoms in a dense bush of gases. Last year, a supernova lit up in one of its outer arms, though we wouldn't have been able to see it with the naked eye.

Trucks ply the highway amid the sleeker sounds of cars, one

every several minutes. A gap in noise opens between two shrieks racing away from each other, their Doppler shifts trailing off for miles. There should be a word for listening to two vehicles heading opposite directions, their sounds stretching thin till you hear neither. In this near-silent gap, I lay my heart on the water, feeling like I'm standing in space on a Bortle 4 causeway.

The quiet between the car and truck ends with an explosion. A concussion more terrific than the loudest firework erupts high in the air and I'm startled half a step backwards. Coots and herons in the reeds squawk as birds stir up around the lake. Wingbeats strike water. Do I see something up there, maybe a flash of red or yellow or something burning before going out? My senses are scrambled for an instant. We're not on military land, but we're close and the explosion came from above the lake, which is over the Pahranagat National Wildlife Refuge, not a place where military explosives are allowed. It's not unusual in Nevada or other parts of the Southwest, but with a jolt to my heart, tonight it's unusual to me. The echoes strike off mountains, the sound of range after range spreading outward, and half a minute later a similar blast goes off much farther away. Its echoes ripple as if one bomb were talking to another.

We haven't witnessed anything strange overhead yet, which is odd. Skirting a bombing range for the last two days, we expected peculiar lights in the distance. When Irvin and I worked the lower Colorado River, we were surrounded by bombing ranges and military airspace, and over the years we racked up a variety of gaseous glowing domes of who knows what and flares slowly descending on what must have been parachutes, evidence of nighttime maneuvers on the ground. On this bike ride, we've only seen jet fighters twisting around each other thousands of feet overhead, engines roaring to push one ahead of the next, each designed to blow the other up. That's a daily thing. At night, we see their thrusters flaring like bright blue eyes.

Through reeds and cattails with their spear-edged leaves, I hurry back to camp. My green lamp makes my path seem more haunting as I wonder what is out here that I don't expect or even comprehend, and wouldn't this be the perfect place for roots to snake out of the mud and grab my feet to drag me under, never to be seen again? Or perhaps something mysterious in a military way, an experimental tractor beam? Who knows what that explosion set off in my head? I figured I'd be freaked out by thoughts of aliens and encampments of meth addicts when we were in the middle of nowhere, and now that we're near a highway, I'm thumbing through a rack of horror movie plots like old DVDs. The world feels safer away from people. The explosion unnerved me; it's the loudest thing I've heard since Vegas.

When I get back to camp, Irvin is awake in his bag. I say what the hell was that and he says it was crazy. In the dark I can hear his smile, and I'm relieved. It's good to have a friend by your side, rather than sitting alone at a picnic table with satellites criss-crossing overhead. We exchange notes and decide that it had to be a military-grade ordnance designed to frighten and disorient rather than destroy. Which, if that's true, it worked. Then Irvin says that he saw something strange in the sky.

"Strange?"

"It was moving like a satellite, but then it changed direction and changed color."

"Changed direction?"

"It turned course. I don't see how that could happen, but it did. Or maybe I didn't see it. I'm not sure."

I press for more, but that's all he's got. It happened shortly after the explosion, and he knows it wasn't a plane or a helicopter, its passage utterly silent. I must not have noticed because I was hurtling through the reeds, trying not to stumble in lake water or get eaten by monsters.

About forty miles due west of here is Area 51, about which I know next to nothing. The nearness of the famously secretive military facility might get UFO folks excited, but I can't say I'm one. As a stargazer, I've seen some odd and inexplicable lights in the sky, but they've almost always been near military ranges. They remain, at least to me, inexplicable, so yes, you could say I've seen unidentified flying objects. But when it comes to aliens and such, I'm no authority. We might as well flip the coin on whether we are the only ones looking around in this absurdly vast universe. As Arthur C. Clarke wrote, "Two possibilities exist: either we are alone in the Universe or we are not. Both are equally terrifying."

My mother's parents first met at an airbase in Marfa, Texas, during World War II, and from there people have long claimed seeing the famed and mysterious Marfa Lights. My dad was born two hundred miles almost due north of there in Roswell one year after the first nuclear bomb test just over the horizon, and one year before what is claimed to be the crash of an extraterrestrial spaceship just outside of town, which sparked an industry of conspiracy theories. I am of Southwest alien ilk, like it or not. We see life from a different orbit, strange things common in the sky. Look through a telescope at a nebula blossoming like a flower, with stars being born inside it, and do so with the knowledge that their light is taking hundreds to millions of years to reach us, and that is strange enough.

Bortle 3

* * * * * * * * * *

Some indication of light pollution is evident along the horizon. Clouds may appear faintly illuminated in the brightest parts of the sky near the horizon but are dark overhead. The Milky Way appears complex, and globular clusters such as M4, M5, M15, and M22 are all distinct naked-eye objects. M33 is easy to see with averted vision. The zodiacal light is striking in spring and autumn (when it extends 60° above the horizon after dusk and before dawn) and its color is at least weakly indicated.

* * * * * * * * * *

BORTLE 3

The highway pitches us where we don't want to be. There are guardrails but no shoulders, and the way tightens until we have to get off and walk. Semitrucks thunder past as we push bikes along the backside of a guardrail for a quarter mile, brisk morning wind smacking from every fly-by. This is a path the odd travel, a trail barely set, the ground sprayed with hunks of asphalt and pieces of truck tire, plastic hubcaps shot off at high speed and broken into shrapnel. I'm thinking we should have continued due north with the water we had, but we probably would have failed and ended up here anyway. This is the place of dead animals, a couple of dogs that tires obliterated by the time they landed off the highway, and something with fur we can't identify. Cat? Squirrel? I hold up a mummified snake split head to tail, its ribs exposed like an open zipper.

We reach the highway town of Alamo and veer immediately to the town grocery-deli-gas station. At midweek lunchtime, the high school crowd is here, fathers and sons in pickup trucks, teenagers pulling in, younger kids showing up on bikes or walking in a gang from across the highway. Nobody jeers or stares at us as we sit on a bench next to the automatically sliding door; we receive only what we deserve, politely averted gazes. We don't look like professionals—no sleek trekking outfits—our shirts crusted with salt and dust, bikes leaning against each other like tired horses. The postmistress, still wearing her name tag, is the only person to say hello, and she says it kindly.

I have a quartered fried chicken half the size of my head and a whole pickle to go with it. Salt, meat, fat. Sugar, too; I got lost in the candy aisle for a couple of minutes and came out with a chocolate bar. I don't know what Irvin's eating because I'm not paying attention to him, too much on my own plate. I've got blackberries, too, something alive and sweet to share, a baggie of radishes, and a persimmon—who would have thought you'd find a persimmon in the Alamo grocery store—all laid out on my lap with a napkin as I sit on a bench next to Irvin where every person going in or out of the store has to experience us. We look out at gas pumps under a white and green canopy, red logo, colors as bold as the ones that got me lost in the candy aisle. We count people, watch traffic, and when we're starting to feel ill from everything we've eaten and done to ourselves, we get back on our bikes and pedal out of town. Is this so different from Vegas?

Yes, it's different. The road we're following is the old highway, abandoned and cracked. Grasses are growing through asphalt. Some people live along it, not many—trailers and slapped-up houses with barking dogs and wood-pallet fences. The smell of hay and livestock gives way to an empty half-paved road, with lines painted down the middle no longer useful.

Dead ends and off-road two-tracks lie ahead. We find anything to avoid the highway, getting onto a dirt path and riding up and down a hilly fence line. If highway drivers in passing cars see us from a hundred yards away, we must look like we're pedaling camels with all that we're carrying—two camel pedalers riding the hills and gullies of an OHV route, going straight instead of contouring around the landscape. Some roads should not go straight; they plow through terrain, and either it's cut-and-fill or, like this road, a rollercoaster. I stop at a hilltop and look back, seeing Irvin as a dot about eight hilltops behind me. He's off his bike and working on something; tightening, refitting. It's not a flat, or he'd have the bike on its side. Most of this day will be a hodgepodge, following whatever route we can find. He won't catch up for another ten minutes, so I get off and walk through creosote bushes and the dust of semi-crushed igneous rock. No Joshua trees, we haven't seen any since yesterday afternoon. We must be moving out of their range. Boulders the size of pickup trucks show where bedrock has been exposed and weathered into pieces. Good place to find rock art, I think, not a thought that's gone through my head since the start of the trip. When you wonder something like that, go look.

The sky is a tracing of high thin clouds, blue laundered through a veneer of mares' tails, signs of weather coming. I miss walking. Bikes are getting us far, but they are still machines. The first boulder I reach, flat-bottomed and tipped over, I find awash in petroglyphs of animals and lines going this way and that. *Hello*, I say, both surprised and not at all surprised. With water nearby—a chain of lakes that have been here through all human history—people would have been drawn to the land around these boulders. I'd guess five hundred to seven hundred years old, these come from Paiute ancestors, the older images of bighorn sheep brushed darker by patina possibly Archaic in age, thousands of years.

If I didn't know better, I'd say the lines pecked into the rock show ways of travel. It looks like a map, the lines crossing through each other and wandering around the boulder's hazelnut face. Some of the markings follow natural cracks in the rock as if erosion features are part of whatever landscape the petroglyphs describe.

The next boulder is a stone's throw away. It has a pointed cap being danced around by fanciful bighorn sheep, their bodies arched with heads down as if they're butting. The scene reads like part of a legend, bighorns ringing around a summit, a gathering of some sort.

The night sky these ancient people lived under was Bortle 1. You couldn't shrug off a cosmos like that. Their oldest stories are about stars, and in a Southern Paiute Nuwu creation story from this area, the North Star is a bighorn sheep, Na'gah, the sky god's son. Legend tells of how Na'gah climbed to the top of a steep and perilous mountain, the hardest mountain of all. But the way caved in behind him, and he was trapped. If he tried to go back down, he would die. His father saw this from above and was heartbroken. Instead of letting his son die on the mountaintop, he transformed him into a star and placed him at the pole of the night, the most important of stellar bodies.

In other stories of Nuwu origin, more bighorns followed Na'gah's route upward. Like him, they got stuck, so the sky god placed them around his son where they became what is known, in colonizer-speak, as the Big and Little Dippers. They travel around the wayfinding star of Na'gah, who is always in the middle. I don't know if this is the story I'm reading on the rock, but it seems possible. It looks like a recollection from Creation, the dance of the first stars who were also bighorn sheep. I listen for the boulder, trying to detect sounds of voices, the thud of a hammerstone striking a bone chisel, and singing from old legends, the chanted words of someone telling a story. They are all here.

Irvin catches up, and together we walk from boulder to boulder, finding beds of broken bottle glass and rusted cans approaching a century old. The sun is a soft blanket on our shoulders. It feels good to have our skinny little daypacks off and left on the ground, dropped back by the bikes.

Poking around for more petroglyphs, we find a sunburnt metal carcass of a car, partly buried in a drift of coarse sand. It is a late 1940s, early 1950s model, no glass or parts remaining, not even a steering wheel. It was stripped and left for dead. This is also an artifact and it, too, sounds like voices to me, conversations between people in once-upholstered seats, hands being held, a kiss, a sigh. Someone was proud of this vehicle and kept its paint job shiny.

By 1939, the highway near here would have been paved, so this car would have known the peel of rubber on hot asphalt. Vegas was already growing fast, doubling in size, tripling, but far enough away that it hardly mattered. It was still a long drive until you'd start seeing the glow at night. Alamo, a small farming and ranching community, was half its current population. It was also the nearest town downwind from nearby nuclear bomb testing that started in Nevada in 1951—928 detonations, most of them below ground but some above, leaving desert basins more cratered than the face of the moon. These bomb tests brought glowing dust and a legacy of strange maladies, with cancer clusters sometimes taking out whole families, same here as it was in New Mexico at the time. We once played clumsily with light, seeing how bright we could make it, and went too far. This is a cautionary tale that will also be remembered by our artifacts, the rusty metal skin of this vehicle still tingling from fallout.

Irvin and I stop for pictures along Nevada State Route 375, officially the "Extraterrestrial Highway." There's a roadside business with a hand-painted billboard colored alien-green reading "E.T. FRESH JERKY" and "JERKY FROM AREA 51" with a depiction of cows being pulled into a flying saucer. The state highway sign, poles and all, is plastered with stickers. We're in a vacation slideshow. A rental RV pulls in, and a troop of motorcycles is pulling out. The parking lot is the size of a football field, packed to dust and mostly empty. Across the highway stands a skeletal gray radio tower that we'll see flashing from miles away tonight. The owners of the jerky stand live in Vegas and are rumored to have an air-conditioning business. They put up murals of aliens dressed as cowboys; one has a rifle with smoke coming out of the barrel. Another is pointing as if to let you know something important is happening, but I can't tell what. There seem to be different alien species, one more lizard-like than the others. I pause without getting off my bike, hoping to decipher whatever this story is.

This jerky shack must get strange and dreamy around midnight, when truck traffic dies down and the place is overwhelmed by stars. I'd like it better, then. Something as campy as this could use an upgrade—anchored to the infinite sky while a lonely red light flashes atop the tower across the highway.

I give up on reading anything into the mural. It looks like a postcard from a desert peyote trip.

You can go four directions from here, and we take the more minor, northbound highway. Red flashers are attached to our rears as big trucks boom past us. Sunset gets us to a cattle gate that we lower to roll our bikes through, hooking it back to its wood post with a wire loop, public access as long as you close the gate behind you. A good dirt road takes us out as we bike slowly, looking for a marker. We left a food and water resupply here. We hadn't factored in our gluttony in Alamo when we planned this trip, but that was hours ago, and I'm feeling better now.

The marker we're using is a dead steer. It's been on the ground for a while, hide turned into a drum, bare white bones poking out where they've torn through. Fifty feet off the road, it's not hard to spot. We drop bikes when we get to the carcass. Joshua trees have faded away, and creosote bushes once close enough to touch each other are now spaced a hundred feet apart. We are crossing from the Mojave Desert into the cooler, higher Great Basin Desert, where plants are a little tougher and lower to the ground. Stiff bushes—blackbrush, greasewood, Mormon tea—look like sea urchins creeping across an ocean floor.

When we originally set this cache, we weren't sure which direction we might be coming from, or how late or early in the trip it might be. We wanted to be prepared for any eventuality. The cache was put here like a planet we could spin around, using its gravity to slingshot ourselves to our final destination in the next basin ahead. It holds dried mangos, energy bars, extra meals, and a tin of homemade ginger cookies that my editor baked and sent with us, along with a few cans of dark brown ale, the same kind we tried to down back at the last cache. We'd hauled this cache into a gully: seven gallons of water and three plastic paint buckets packed tight and sealed with duct tape. While placing these, I had jumped into the gully so Irvin could hand me two cardboard boxes of supplies, when a rattlesnake broke into a skin-crawling buzz. I backed away as far as I could, which was only a few feet inside the gully. A three-foot-long western diamondback lay half wound up in the rocky bank across from me. It was young, but old enough to have grown buttons on its tail. I spoke softly to it as Irvin said, matter-of-factly, *we have our protector*. The rattling subsided, but the snake was now on edge, looped back around itself and ready to strike. As I brought one of the boxes down, it shot out with fangs bared, almost hitting the box. I said, *peace little one, peace, we'll be gone soon enough.* I don't know if soothing a snake with your voice works, but it helped me. Once everything was placed, I hopped right out.

This time, Irvin goes down first to retrieve our cache, leaning ahead to see around rocks. I stay above to receive, saying, "Maybe it's back in the boxes. Give it a kick, see if it rattles."

I've seen Irvin dodge strikes before; I know his body posture, a little more weight on his back leg for a spring in the opposite direction. He reaches in and grabs a gallon jug, pulling it out: No rattle, no snake.

Now it's beer-and-cookie time, anything we want. The deli-gas station debauchery prepared us, and I'm trying to decide how to do the appetizer, bite of cookie, sip of beer, or the other way around? A hearty dinner follows, rice and dehydrated meat and sauce reconstituted with boiled water, the food of astronauts.

Irvin says he's paring down here, leaving half of his gadgetry behind and we'll pick it up when we come back through, cleaning up our caches on the other end of the trip. "Let's take enough food and water to reach the Bortle," he says, and I agree. That's what we've come to call our destination, the Bortle, the darkest of the dark. Friends are scheduled to meet us in a couple days and shuttle us back to where we started. From here we'll make our last shot, light and fast.

Alamo is small enough that from twenty miles away its light

doesn't count for much, and Vegas is still the brightest light-form we can see. It's smaller than it has been but it's not budging, the core of its radiance now the size of a grape held at arm's length. Clouds rise over the distant city and their appearance doubles the brightness, a mantle of reflected light. I wave my fingers over a blank journal page, and the shadow is still there. We're a hundred miles away by line of sight, 150 on our bikes, and Vegas still casts a shadow. The stars don't seem influenced, scattershot Milky Way starting to look like an arm of a galactic disk. Interstellar clouds lie luxuriantly through its middle as if stretched out on a lounge. One could sketch the structure of this Milky Way and it would make sense.

Every night our camp is at a different angle to the basins and the ranges around us, and I have to turn the sky in my mind to figure out where I am. Quickly locating constellations is harder now, swamped by thousands of stars, making counting them beyond impossible. Constellation viewing is better in a Bortle 5, where major features stand out. Now space is becoming soup—Big Bang material, the Milky Way sitting in back, all visible stars in front of it. Jupiter is up close and bulging subtly, even to the naked eye, where its moons are making themselves known.

Downy little patches of nebulas are out tonight, surrounded by space glow the color of salt water. The Orion Nebula is a delicate smear of luminescent fog seated in our arm of the Milky Way. When the solar-orbiting James Webb telescope turned its gaze to the heart of this nebula, it revealed 540 free-floating giant planets disconnected from any solar systems, some of them orbiting each other, others wandering off alone. These were reported a month before we started our trip, and astronomers were puzzling over where these exoplanets came from and whether solitary Jupiter-sized bodies are common in our galaxy. Are they stars that didn't have the mass to make it, duds spit out of the stellar nursery, or were they ejected from their own solar systems? When I heard of this find, I thought of how strange it must be for a planet to have no sun, no daytime, none of our airglow or zodiacs. What it would have is a perpetual view of hot, glowing folds, a full 360 degrees of many-colored space clouds inside the nebula. The view might feel comforting, as if from within the chambers of a stellar nautilus light-years across.

Our view from Earth is from a midway arm in what is classified as a barred spiral galaxy, our solar system lying 26,000 light-years from the Milky Way's star-dense center. Closer to that center, a night sky would be flush with light from not thousands but millions of stars. The night depends entirely on where you are. Ours is a relatively diffuse perspective, with our Northern and Southern Hemispheres looking at their own compliments of stars in different directions. South has its Magellanic Clouds, a pair of irregular dwarf galaxies orbiting outside of the Milky Way and plainly visible, like two luminous cotton balls. I'm envious of the south having these two marvelous features. While there's no pole star in the south, robust constellations circling tightly around the pole serve the same purpose. When I've traveled south of the equator, I couldn't get used to seeing Orion, a constellation shared by both hemispheres, turned upside-down. The concept of Orion the bold hunter falls apart when it's flipped the other way. It doesn't look the same. What we in the north call the belt and sword, in Australia is called the saucepan.

There is no X-marks-the-spot, no center of the universe, no one place from which to see. The story we witness in the sky is told only for this solar system, no one else. Travel elsewhere in the galaxy and it will look different. Constellations distort over great distances until they are unrecognizable.

Beyond the limits of galaxies there exist isolated stars, possibly with their own lonely solar systems left from galaxies passing close or through each other and losing bits of themselves as they go by. One such star was identified 300,000 light-years from anything else. If it has a planet, the panorama at night would be vacuous, smudges, if anything, of faraway galaxies so diminished they shine as if through wool. What would that have done to us to have no stars, only the local siblings, sun and moon, and our few visible planets following each other? We'd know nothing of the bigger family tree and its blinding abundance. If I'd been a child left on a mattress in the woods, I may not have found affinity in a dark and empty sky. I might have fallen into despair. Knowing how fortunate we are, how could we blot it out?

From my dad I used to hear about mysterious sounds in the night. He was prone to talking about such things. I was young when he first described this supposed phenomenon, the music of the spheres, reflecting on what ancient thinkers believed they were hearing in the night sky, the likes of Pythagoras and Ptolemy. Music in early Greece was as much a science as astronomy. It was a way of understanding mathematical relationships and the audible harmonies they produce.

A theory among the early Greeks was that the planets and stars made sound that a person could hear—*Musica universalis*. This came from perfect mathematical steps between orbiting bodies translated into notes, as if the solar system were an instrument. When the air is still and quiet, perhaps you've heard it, or thought you have. Sitting alone in the Utah desert under a full moon, I swear I picked up a wavering pitch sung as if by a boys' choir, a single triumphal chord at the edge of auditory range. To the ancient Greeks and to my dad, it would have been obvious what I was hearing.

Aristotle found this idea preposterous. In the 4th century BC, he wrote, "Melodious and poetical as the theory is, it cannot be a true account of the facts."

As it turns out, Aristotle may have been wrong. Of course, we can't hear through outer space, but our sun emits pressure waves that equate to sound in the form of chirps and garbles and a powerful, ceaseless roar. It is assumed that all stars do the same, like whales sounding in the deep. The Chandra X-ray Observatory, which orbits the Earth, focused its mirrors on a black hole in the Perseus Cluster and recorded rings of pressure waves rippling outward through gas clouds. Read like grooves on a vinyl disk, the ripples from the black hole's emissions have been converted into what sounds like a howling wind of instruments playing so far into the bass that humans couldn't hear it, fifty-seven octaves below middle C. This is not necessarily the universal music that so many Greeks believed in, but it is a form of sound, and it adds up, coming from all directions.

My dad, who ended up an insurance salesman in Phoenix, took me to a *Star Trek* convention back in my elementary school days at my request, and he seemed glad to go along with it. In a convention hall, he watched the original 1956 *Forbidden Planet* with me, and he bought me an Isaac Asimov book entitled "Cosmic Catastrophes." He had to have been a little proud, a fan of the heavens and Greek astronomers, seeing his kid all starry-eyed. When Carl Sagan came on TV with his COSMOS show, we sat on the couch rapt by Sagan's mouthwatering billions and billions.

When my dad and I camped just the two of us, he would sit at our fire drinking whiskey or beer or both, talking about pulsars and neutron stars. He told me to be quiet and listen to the sky, and I would. Maybe it was his growing up in a clump of lights in a dark hole of New Mexico that made him this way, or a galactic curiosity in the genes he passed on to me. A junior or senior from Roswell High, driving a candy-red Chevy to what is known as the Bottomless Lakes outside of town, he lived in a halo of Bortle 1 extending as far as he'd ever been, a place so empty it engendered a rich lore of aliens. There was no direction he could look without facing a gulf of nothing.

I imagine him as a lanky teenager, a track star with his picture in the paper, strolling to the edge of one of the freshwater cenotes in the dark past town with his arm around his date's shoulder, likely my mom. They'd stop to look up at the starfield with a reflection in the water forming a perfect mirror, heaven on Earth. "You hear that?" he would say. "That's the music of the spheres."

Our oldest stories are about stars. The current popular telling is scientific and relies on how features like the Orion Nebula and other stellar nurseries produce bright new suns: compression, heat, nuclear fusion, *voila!* For a much longer time, we lived under a different imagining, a prodigious sky not necessarily bound to science but loaded with conversation and rabble, bickering celestial relatives, the Morning Star chasing the moon and slipping behind her orb. Deities got revenge on each other while playing with us mortals down on the ground. For its permanence and eternal shine, nothing was stationary up there. Legends showed agency in the night sky, not just spheres of mass and radiation slinging around each other, but a brilliant and brawling presence.

When Irvin and I worked with kids on the river, a campfire favorite was recounting traditional tales of how the world came to be, how animals formed mountains, or raccoon ended up with a bandit mask on its face. Having studied mythic cosmology in college, I came to the job with stories from around the world. Coyote Scatters the Stars was one I often dipped into. This is a Diné legend, Navajo tradition, a mostly Athabaskan heritage that arrived in the Four Corners with a preexisting relationship with stars. I've read and heard different versions, and in the end, it's always the same: stars strewn wildly across the heavens by the hand of Trickster Coyote.

Around the fire, I'd tell the kids about how a deity known as Haashch'ééshzhiní—Black God—took the stars from a buckskin pouch and placed them in the heavens. He thought long on his arrangements, positioning each with care. He'd step back like an artist to study his composition, considering how it was coming along, and I'd play this part up, pretending I was Haashch'ééshzhiní, holding a star between thumb and forefinger as if it were a precious gem, pondering where to put it. We had an actual sky for reference, which helped, and some kids weren't watching me or the fire, but sat back on their elbows looking up as if they couldn't take their eyes off the sky.

Along comes Coyote trotting, doing his fancy dance, getting the attention of Haashch'ééshzhiní, saying *Hey, what's that pouch of magic glowing crystals you got?* I'd dance around as I told this part, pretending I had a tail and a needle-nose snout. Haashch'ééshzhiní told him to get out of here. Coyote couldn't resist and he stole the pouch, taking off running with Black God coming after him like a storm yelling, *no, Coyote, no!*

Coyote reached into the pouch and threw the stars up so hard they stuck and stayed wherever they landed, threw them until all the stars were spent. Coyote then dug deeper into the pouch and pulled out powder gathered at the bottom. He hurled that powder with all his might and formed the Milky Way, which was my cue to reach into my pocket and pull up a fistful of lemonade powder I'd pinched from the food supplies. I'd throw the powder into the fire and it would explode into a plume of rainbow colors lighting up the faces of kids. When the flash wore down, darkness filled in, and the sky opened like a theater over their heads, all the stars exactly where Coyote left them.

I loved that story. Though it's not from my forebears, it made sense to me, its concept universal. In scientific fields, it would be called *self-organization* categorized under the study of *chaos theory*. There are unstable elements in the universe and they act as forces of creation by shaking up old equilibria, bringers of stars and everything we know by making a mess of things. Without disarray, there would be no array.

In a high desert canyon northeast of Wellington, Utah, patina on sandstone has been pecked into the form of Coyote standing upright like a person. With its head turned in profile, this anthropomorphic animal holds what appears to be a pouch, which is likely the pouch that held all the stars at the beginning of time. Surrounding this petroglyph is a grid of hundreds of distinctly circular peck marks, which are understood to represent the night sky. The rock art panel is more than a thousand years old and appears to recount Coyote creating the heavens, which is how I've come to believe it actually happened.

Irvin starts a fire and we stand closely around it, crushing out sparks that land beyond the rock ring we've made, me using my treaded shoe soles, Irvin his flip-flops, desert-style. We'll scuttle and scatter the rocks come morning. Unintentionally, we're still facing toward Vegas, but it's finally vanishing, becoming a faint nebula of itself. We're not staring directly at it because the rest of the sky takes our attention. There are a few ranch lights, but not many, and a single red bulb flashes several miles away, the tip of the radio tower across from the jerky stand on the highway. Irvin says a shroud of dark has been rising and taking over the night, becoming more powerful. The sky is now an entity in itself, and the progress night by night is more noticeable than he thought it would be. It almost feels aggressive, with the night finally winning. Irvin cups the air with his hands, packing down the light of Vegas like a snowball. Soon nothing will be left of it.

On the meter, I get a magnitude 21.4, a good Bortle 3. Stars are rich and numberless. How could this view be understood as anything but living? Stars are born bright and hot, most of their lives spent in middle-aged stability, like our own sun shining with little variation. Some famously turn blue or red and swell into giants, either erupting in cardiac explosions or shrinking, dimming, and finally going out. What looks like a static field is a problem of time. We'd be led to believe that nothing much changes up there, but we're not around long enough to recognize how stars are drifting and coming on, going out. If our perceptions were set to an astronomical timescale, everything would be in motion as our solar system corkscrews through the Milky Way at half a million miles per hour. The question of are we alone is answered by a view full of stars. We are so not alone it isn't funny.

Those who study the history of our galaxy through its shapes and elemental fingerprints are called *galactic archaeologists,* a title that has to be a pleasure to drop in conversation, the Indiana Jones of astrophysicists. These are scientists who study chemical abundance signatures in stars and extrapolate where they came from, basically using stellar features the way regular archaeologists use artifacts or bones, piecing them back together as they once were. A star's chemistry has scarcely changed since it first formed and can be grouped with others, telling which blasted out of one nebula or another and then mixed into the Milky Way's swirl. The content of a star will show its age, if it was formed early in the galactic disk or more recently, which adds a dimension of time to the dimension of space. The Milky Way is a map pinned with strings connecting stars back and forth to their sources, and this is a way of seeing stellar evolution.

An astrophysicist might see the Milky Way overhead as a sort of artifact that can be studied in order to piece galactic history back together, metal-rich near its bright center and lighter in molecules in the extended halo. At times, I've seen it as stardust Coyote hurled into the sky, or, as the name suggests, a river of milk. It is a facet of the night sky that begs explanation, a structure that suggests more is going on up there than just infinite stars. To see it is to know we live within a composition that extends for hundreds of thousands of light-years. We are seeing the very edifice of our galaxy, something no human being, or beetle, or bird, should miss.

BORTLE 2

* * * * * * * * * * *

Airglow may be weakly apparent along the horizon. M33 is rather easily seen with direct vision. The summer Milky Way is highly structured to the unaided eye, and its brightest parts look like veined marble when viewed with ordinary binoculars. The zodiacal light is still bright enough to cast weak shadows just before dawn and after dusk, and its color can be seen as distinctly yellowish when compared with the blue-white of the Milky Way. Any clouds in the sky are visible only as dark holes or voids in the starry background.

* * * * * * * * * * *

BORTLE 2

S trike this day from the record. It won't count on my chart. Since morning, we've had solid cloud cover, a ceiling down to ten thousand feet and dropping. Many-colored mountains have shifted toward the grayer parts of the spectrum. In this light, they look softer, kinder. The West is famed for its quality of light, and I appreciate the clarity, orizons etched as if with acid. A deep, rain-bearing gray like this is a remarkable contrast. Sunglasses aren't needed, the eye of the sky no longer on top of us.

Signs of human presence have dribbled away, a few gray houses scattered along the dirt side roads that we don't take. When I come to a turn along a graded stem of a road, Irvin shouts from behind which route to take. He's watching on his screen, getting us through a briar patch of private property, bane of wanderers in the West. This is ag land, a gift of the same aquifer that allows the refuge lakes to exist, and as soon as we climb over the next rumple of mountains, we'll be out of it and back into sheer desert. It's the kind of day that could be called dreary, but it feels like liberation to me.

Our route leads us through ranchlands with cattle guards that rattle our panniers. We pass a barn where trucks are parked, and a couple of guys in cowboy hats lean against a tailgate watching us as we ride through. No wave, no exchange of words, which is fine; if they took note of us, it would most likely mean we were not where we were supposed to be. *County road access* is listed right here on the map. Irvin's ready to defend our presence, using his Forest Service voice, but nobody stops us.

A few miles later, we find that our road veers off to where we're not going. Irvin was afraid this would happen, finding his satellite map unclear. I don't mind, we're making good progress, starting to leave ag lands behind, bound for more exposed and empty places. We walk bikes through open desert—rabbitbrush and tumbleweeds, flat rocky ground, most of a pronghorn's skull, rusted cans half a century old. Hoisting bikes over a barbed wire fence is like trying to pass Shetland ponies to each other. The air smells like water—not like it did back at Pahranagat, with its cottonwoods and greasewood, but like pure water, atmospheric moisture. Tonight we will have rain.

We're now nearing the center of one of the darkest zones in the country, but we're not there yet, and tonight it will be smothered by weather. Satellite imagery tells us we've been in a Bortle 1 for a couple days, which is not the case. Bortle 1 is still ahead.

A few months earlier I'd visited the north side of this night island, which is roughly the length of Cuba stretching from outside of Las Vegas well into Oregon. My wife and I drove through Oregon's Steens Mountains and the hardpacked Alvord Desert, where, on the parched, chalky floor, we camped out of the back of our car. This was at a bubbling, hissing hot spring with no one around, empty because the water is too hot to enjoy, a skin-peeling temperature. We positioned ourselves in a pair of folding chairs with a bottle of whiskey and two cups on the ground where we could watch stars emerge. Springs jabbered and sputtered through holes, a little desert Yellowstone serenading the nightfall, which took about an hour to come to full summer fruition. We treated the event like a long, slow fireworks display, calling out the first star, the second, and the third. If it were a drinking game, we'd have been done for. At ten stars she said there's always a lull about now. "Ten stars…ten stars…ten stars," she said, looking for another to add. A minute later I said, "Twelve." She countered, "Sixteen." The lull was over and now they came fast. Wish after wish, we continued until we couldn't wish anymore. The last stage of twilight was like a snap, Earthlight gone, heavens reaching their capacity. Suddenly, we were floating in an immense cosmos as cracks in the Earth steamed loudly around us, as if we'd drifted back to the start of it all. I got up in the middle of the night and walked among the boiling pots, and the sky was laid bare, five or six satellites passing by at all times, meteorites every few minutes. Even if you don't know what you're seeing, names of stars and numbers of light-years, the knowledge of another side to this coin, the up to our down, is enough.

Gray military transports jets fly in low. We stop to watch as one after the next, three in total, roar through the mountains under a deck of clouds and, wings tilting, vanish from sight. When they are gone, we keep moving.

Irvin's got a route on his map marked "old highway." It's not much of a highway; there's not a chunk of asphalt left on this roughly driven two-track, just dried buckwheat bulbs and soft-headed rabbitbrush growing in the middle. It was probably never paved, a highway that's been here for a hundred years, still used from time to time. The air feels like winter's coming; snow will be on the peaks tonight. Our elevation smells of rain. Precipitation is up there somewhere, thousands of feet above us, but the desert air is not yet letting it through. The old highway leads to a fine, graded road, meant for traffic, but there's none to be seen, not a vehicle for an hour and then two. Winding through brown toothy ridges that casually shrug off their boulders, we pass into rock gaps and butte lands. When we top out, we're looking into the next basin, the largest we've seen, twenty-two miles across, cooked down into the extinct Pleistocene color of a boiled egg.

Irvin kicks into his pedals and charges his bike ahead as if going into battle, shouting, "To the Bortle!" I kick in right behind him.

The road is a gentle downhill for many miles following the long slope of the basin, the lightest pedaling putting us on a magic carpet. The ceiling looks like a watercolor quilt of clouds, and the horizon stretches to infinity. After an hour, we stop for an ass break and walk for a quarter mile, pushing our bikes along the road. "We're back in silence," Irvin says. "It's wonderful."

We both stop to listen. No crunch of tires, or sound of our shoes plodding, or gear on our bikes rattling and shifting. Even last night we could hear air brakes in the distance, truck traffic far away. These last couple of days, coming back in range of a highway, made us appreciate the quiet that lies farther out, a muteness that has texture.

The silence of this final basin echoes across the miles. We're off the night sky map tonight; no view of space awaits us, clouds sealing off every horizon. I'm suddenly freed by the thought, released from a journal loaded with the names of constellations and stars, notes on what's visible, what's not, cross-referenced to John Bortle's scale. I was starting to get bug-eyed. I've heard ancient Polynesian navigators could be identified by the bags under their eyes from nights of staring from a boat deck while others slept. I suspect I have at least a sliver of bags by now. A night off will be good.

Back on our bikes in the cool breeze of descent, I feel as if I could spread my arms wide, so I do, letting the bike ride itself, cool air pouring across my face. Irvin blazes past me, laughing.

This will be our darkest night, I already know that. We'll have complete cloud coverage and no shadows from anywhere. The light meter won't be trustworthy. Tonight, I want the night to overpower Vegas and grind it like a cigarette butt under its heel.

Unlike so many environmental dilemmas we face—extinctions, destabilized climates, and sea level rises that could take decades, centuries, or forever to halt or reverse—the problem of artificial light and the killing of night is a relatively simple fix. Light is a pollutant that vanishes with the flip of a switch.

Night sky advocacy is on the rise as people realize what we're losing, how fast it's happening, and how straightforward it is to reverse. Communities around the world scramble for designations. A Chamber of Commerce loves astrotourism, another way of getting people to visit. In Colorado, I live in a registered Bortle 1, a pocket beyond the light-sheds of small and distant cities where my county added lighting codes, and the nearest town of five hundred people did the same. This happened with little to no pushback, surprising in an area ripe with gun nuts and berry-picking radicals. The kinds of people who usually come to public meetings throwing up their hands about government control had nothing to say. The value of night in our dark corner seemed to be agreed upon.

Kris Holstrom, one of our county commissioners, told me she'd encountered only one person visibly angry about dark sky regulations, a guy who wadded up an information sheet and threw it away in front of her. She expected a lot more resistance. "I was surprised how well people warmed up," she said. "They go along with it because it's a good idea. Those harsh lights are just gnarly. Once they get some education, which is hugely important, people start to see that it's a much more pleasant place because it's not as bright."

Kris has a kind and powerful face, the expression of an intense listener. She sat at my kitchen table with Ellen Metrick, the new board president of the local dark sky alliance. Creighton Wood—or Woody, as we call him—was here, too. He's an amateur astronomer and a rancher who was part of the initial push to have our town designated as an International Dark Sky Community, and now we have signs on the highway on either end of town proclaiming the honorific. This is what a local dark sky advocacy gathering looks like. Kris weighed in with what's at stake, Woody reported on how it's going, and Ellen listened in and tried to figure out what she's supposed to be doing in her new volunteer position. We're friends, all on a first-name basis. This is how preservation works at this scale, small places tending to their inheritance.

Woody is a tall man with a brisk white beard, his fingers knotted from work on his sheep and alpaca ranch. He said, "I did notice that Sam's Service Station cut the lights in their canopy. There's still some light, but I'm impressed. That's one of the leading causes of light pollution, you know? Parking lots, gas stations, places like that stay open all night, especially for the service of vehicles, because you've got to see the parking lots. Those reflect everything right back up."

My wife sat on the sofa in front of the wood stove, typing her own work on her laptop. The meeting was at our house, scaled down from the larger night-island cooperatives around the West. When dusk faded and we were still busy talking, she brought candles and an oil lamp to the table and turned off the electric fixture above us. We laughed because we hadn't been conscious of night falling outside. She said you're welcome and went back to the sofa.

You forget when you're indoors and everything is lit to perfection. Hell could break loose in the sky, and we might not notice, carried away by conversation. I asked how they did it, how they were able to get night sky protections for our little town, a redneck libertarian bastion where people bristle at being told what to do. Woody said, "We talked up energy savings and therefore money savings. We talked up wildlife. We talked up human health. And we talked up heritage"—Woody nodded toward Kris whose family had been in the region for almost a century—"what the sky looked like when your folks moved here way back in the 1800s."

Ellen, the alliance president, is a stargazer herself. She and her partner have star names for each other. "It's hard to argue against night skies, just on principle," she said.

When she was fifteen, Ellen worked summers at a mountain lake. One night, she took out a johnboat with some friends, covering its floor with life vests so they could lie on their backs and look up. It was during the Perseid meteor shower, and in a bed of personal floatation devices they got a heavy show. She thinks this should be available to everyone, accessible right out of the sky, free as rain. "Oh my god, that changed my life," she said. "I get chills just thinking about it. I don't know if it was a specifically spectacular year, or the place, or a combination, but we spent the night on the lake and we didn't sleep because it was raining stars the entire night. It was unbelievable. After that, I was hooked."

Woody said, "Nothing I've seen anywhere in the world compares to a frozen-clear January night in the west end." The rest of us agreed, thinking of winter with stars so crisp it feels like you can reach up and pluck them with your fingertips. Those are the nights you step outside, even on the streets of town, and look up. No matter how hard-hearted someone living around here is, you'd mutter to yourself, Jesus, look at that sky.

In our community, the night sky is a bit of a love fest. The town library has a wall dedicated to it with plaques and a stunningly crisp picture of the Andromeda Galaxy taken through a telescope from Woody's property. The photographer is an Astronomer Emeritus at the National Solar Observatory on the other side of the state and he came by invitation to rate our Bortle. While taking long exposures just before midnight, he commented that the few clouds in the sky were not lit at all from below and he told Woody he was impressed, this kind of darkness with a small town nearby is rare. His photograph came from sixty-two two-minute exposures, and when he returned home to process the image, he found one of the finest renditions of the galaxy he had ever taken. Not long after that, with efforts from local advocates, this small town joined a short list of twenty-two communities worldwide officially ranked as the darkest.

West of here, next county over, life is another notch grittier, and night sky issues are not getting the same traction. It's a ranching and former uranium-mining town about twenty minutes closer to the Utah border, where I've been talking with Galit Korngold, who owns a funky little health food store. She describes herself as an open-minded Jewish Canadian liberal from Montreal, and she's been part of the movement to get a night sky designation for her community. Hebrew is her native tongue, and with an accent that sounds vaguely French, her vowels purified and long, she said, "I would love, as the town grows, for it to adopt light ordinances to keep it the way things are at the moment, where we can still see the sky."

Galit has been married for ten years to Kirk Yerke, who is currently mayor of her small town, and who also has an accent that stands out around here, coming originally from Louisiana. He's brazenly opposed to light regulations and votes against them whenever they come to the table. Galit calls her husband a Southern redneck conservative, one of those guys who just won't budge. They have a curious marriage, coming from different worlds with significantly different values, a microcosm of global issues. She told me, "Last night we started talking about this issue and he said, listen, this is my right to have whatever lights I want and I fought for that right in Desert Storm. Are you saying I did that for nothing? And I say, so I don't have the right not to have someone's bright light shining into my bedroom? What about my right to see the night sky?"

I talked to Kirk over the phone and asked as mayor what he would vote for when it came to lighting. "Nothing," he said. "Ever." His voice was calm and rhythmic, not at all angry. He said he speaks for people who think the night sky is not broken around here, so it does not need to be fixed.

He said, "What are we, 2,500 people, in an eight- or nine-mile radius? Let's say a hundred years from now uranium popped up and went crazy, we could grow to 25,000 people. How much light would that be? We still wouldn't compare."

I asked what he thought of the night sky itself, and he repeated what his wife told me: He's in bed by eight or nine o'clock, and the night sky doesn't mean much to him. I talked with Kirk to hear what night sky advocates are up against. "No matter what, you wouldn't have to go but a couple miles out of town to get the skies you want," he said. "Hell, you can see them right now on Main Street."

If the town wanted lighting restrictions, he said, he'd step down. But the town, he said, doesn't want this. "I don't push my views on somebody," he said. "People can put on airport lights if they want. I'm not trying to be a dick. You're talking about a regular porch light, old screw-in bulbs. There are old people who won't buy anything but a fifty-seven-cent lightbulb till the day they die, and you're trying to make choices for those people."

When I asked how he and Galit were managing to pull off a marriage, he seemed unfazed. He said, "She goes out there and takes her light readings. And I can tell she loves it, but I don't have to change my mind."

Galit said she can't get through her husband's head the reason night skies matter. She said, "For these people, their right to do what they want is more important to them than keeping our dark skies."

In this dark hole near the middle of Nevada, nobody is quarreling about night conservation. There are no stationary lights to argue about. The only ones to appear are headlights ten miles away, three vehicles strung out, a mile between each. They're coming from an enormous earthworks art installation in the next basin over, a lifetime project by Nevada-born artist Michael Heizer. It is called, simply, City, in the way that the projection orb in Vegas is called, simply, Sphere. The headlights must be workers or visitors.

The headlights take ten minutes to reach us across this pale, sunken part of the planet and its burden of clouds. Categories of twilight are out the window, it's just darker, and darker, and darker. Our headlamps are on so vehicles will see us coming, otherwise we'd be traveling unlit. A pickup roars past spitting rocks, and another follows. A minute later, an older model four-door slows and stops and the door opens because, I imagine, the window isn't working. In the half-light of his ghostly dashboard, a man leans out and asks if we know where we are and are we ok? He doesn't unbuckle to get out of the car, it's just a courtesy stop. We say yes, we do know, and we're ok. He replies that we're expecting a cold night. We laugh in response. He doesn't.

"You got what you need?" he asks. When we tell him yes, he says, "You sure you don't need help?"

The air is barely moving, not a trace of wind. If anything, cloud cover makes it warmer. The man, however, is worried about rain and bluster, telling us again that the night will be awful, we really don't want to be out here. Maybe he can't imagine sleeping in this basin, how lonely it would be with the eye of the entire night sky upon you. Astrophobia is a real thing. We thank him and say we've been out for days, and we are aware if it rains hard, we might be stranded for a while. These basins can fill with a few inches of water extending as far as can be seen in all directions, meaning Irvin and I would wake on an immense mirror. That wouldn't be bad either, stuck for days on a mirage, licking the last scraps from the inside of a salmon skin bag.

We ask where he's coming from and he says he works at City. I say we've heard of it. His engine is running, headlights aiming at nothing. He tells us there's no place to stay, and the installation is far enough away we wouldn't make it. This is no ragtag backyard project. Building costs for City were $40 million on an installation a mile long by half a mile wide.

In pictures I've seen of it, City looks like Mayans, Greeks, Egyptians, and Chacoans got together and designed a legendary complex thousands of years after the height of their civilizations, and no one lives in it. Covering 704,000 acres, this giant art installation of shaped earth and concrete has the interconnected elegance of a crop circle made to look like a circuit board. Construction started in 1970, and only this year has it been deemed finished and open for viewing.

He's probably worried he'd have to deal with us in the morning—that he'd clock in for the day, whatever his work is, stumbling on us having camped in the center of Heizer's temple illegally. Motion detectors would have gotten us before then, and it's a long drive for a sheriff. He again says how cold it is, and we reassure him we'll be fine. He's not convinced, but he says, "Okay," and wishes us well before closing his door and driving on.

The sound of his car trails away. In this new quiet, I ask Irvin, "Where are we?"

Irvin's face lights up as he taps the phone console strapped between his handlebars, no signal, but he's got maps downloaded. "A couple more miles to the Bortle Hole," he says.

The Bortle Hole is something we'd spotted from aerial imagery. The guy who stopped probably knew it by heart, one of the few markers on this long, dusty commute from one basin to another. It's an abandoned cattle tank and it forms the open mouth of a circle a hundred feet across, one of a few scattered out here. We picked the largest as our stop for the night.

I push into my pedals and start up, Irvin does the same, with less enthusiasm now that the day is over and far-off mountains we've been using for bearings have turned to nothing. Full dark isn't for another hour, some daylight still left, handfuls of photons stretched over miles. We've switched our green and red lights off, a pleasure to be floating through pointillist blue at a firm pedal, no rise, no fall, no change in terrain or direction, road straight and wide. Satellites calibrate themselves on high-albedo basins like this, finding baselines for their distance to the ground. With almost no variability, these basins are some of the flattest places on Earth.

In the last light of astronomical twilight—if this purple-blackness could be called twilight—we glimpse the Bortle Hole, a berm pushed up with a bulldozer into a topographic loaf. When he was first surveying for a location, Heizer would have seen this half-a-century-old hillock set into a perfect man-made circle. I imagine he walked out to it, because there's nothing else to walk out to, strolling its perimeter rim and thinking to himself what could be done in one of these lonely basins. There's a rarely opened wire gate nearby that we unhook and let ourselves through. The ground is parched and cracked into polygons, nothing living but a few greasewood bushes, and even they are having a hard time. We walk bikes up onto the earthen circle where a pastry-like substance you'd be hard-pressed to call soil has been eaten bare by cows and killed by natural sodas and evaporites in this Pleistocene sediment.

The air is still and wanting to rain. The worker from City was right, the night is cold and getting colder. Something's moving in with these clouds, maybe winter. The scent is metallic, and weeks from now this smell will mean snow. If night has fallen or not, we can't tell. I keep thinking this is the extent of the dark, and fifteen minutes later it's darker. My measurements keep climbing past Bortle 1, giving me a magnitude 22.17, which would be Bortle 1+. Ten minutes later, it's a tenth higher. I'm reaching the darkest SQM measurements on record. I give up on meter readings and put up a tent, using my green headlamp while Irvin uses his red lamp to construct his bivvy-tarp, anchoring it to his bike. Shelters have not been part of our nightly rituals. Still, there's some form of natural light. I turn off my lamp and close my eyes for half a minute, a technique for augmenting the adjustment to night vision. When I open them, I move slowly, seeing the tent poles, sliding them into their little grommets, using a scintilla of sky light to find my way.

I thought Vegas would be gone for good, but I scratch its lambent husk from the horizon. It's still there, magnified by clouds hanging low, a glow so soft it's nearly out of the range of vision. We can't seem to get away from it. A new light has appeared in the north: Ely, Nevada, four thousand people, a hundred miles away, fainter than Vegas and in the opposite direction. Both are about as bright as a glow stick popped two days ago, and only the low clouds give them away.

Biking much farther in this direction, we'd find ourselves trapped between new urban glares, Reno and the I-80 corridor splitting this epic lobe of Basin and Range in two. Another reading, just for kicks, lands on 22.38, still darker than the last. I feel like we're disappearing. How does it keep getting darker? I wave my hand over an invisible ground and see a shadow wave in return. Light is coming from above, filtered through clouds. I ask Irvin to try himself, and he verifies by turning off his lamp and waving his hand over the ground. He sees his shadow, too.

Looking up, we can see that the clouds have seams, lines of undulating contact letting foggy lumens through. By now, we're looking at the filtered light of Bortle 2, maybe a Bortle 1. This is as dark as it ever gets on the face of the Earth and it's still not black. I could cup this color in my hands, and slowly, over hours, the cup would fill with a concentrated shadow spilling to the ground. With a ceiling of clouds, this isn't sky-dark. It's another creature, and sky-dark shines through it.

The SQM device I'm using to measure sky light I borrowed from a friend who'd become disillusioned with mainstream dark sky movements. She'd been using it to document her local skies outside of a population 421 town in southern Utah, leading the charge to get the community on an international dark sky registry. Now she tells me that maybe not all dark places should be designated. Some are best left as they are.

Devaki Murch is in her forties and lives outside a high desert town that hardly registers on satellite maps. She's an adoptee who as a baby was airlifted out of Saigon in 1975, and through the vagaries of life has found herself living in one of the darker patches in Utah, no lit-up cities anywhere nearby. Devaki recently joined a small night sky alliance that was trying to get a designation for the community, and her task was to take ambient light recordings, invite observers from DarkSky International, and ultimately get the town its own certificate. She was already a delegate from Utah to the international organization, and it looked like she was bound to succeed in getting her community on the darkness conservation map. But after spending a few months taking her bearings on the topic, talking with community members and chatting with multi-generational ranchers in front of the post office, she withdrew the request. Though her town is in a pristine Bortle 1, she did not feel the place should be put on a registry.

"The reason that they have lights on their barns is that there are wild cats out here," she told me. "There are mountain lions. And when you are an older woman going out to the barn at night, you want those lights on. Totally understood. So would I."

Devaki concluded that there was no need for formal designation. The sky was not broken, and it didn't need fixing. Besides, the issue was too divisive, and the designation appeared to be the opposite of what the community wanted or needed. "Our goal was for people to create relationships with the night," she said. "What I realized when going through the board is that it was not about valuing the night sky and the night for what it is. It was for a designation. You can get a gold designation, a platinum designation, silver designation, whatever designation you frickin' want, but it was an ego thing. It was not about: 'How does this affect the birds?' It was: 'How many houses can you get switched over?' It was all metrics. I said, 'That's not what we're about here.' We're not about metrics. This community will never meet the metric requirements to serve anything. We're tiny. We do not want to be another hit list on the dark sky parks. It's a very private little town and community, and it cherishes the value of the night sky in its isolation and does not want a designation."

Case closed, then, for that town, at least for now. At the current pace of light encroachment, it may be a century or two before light starts crowding its skies—Las Vegas in hyperdrive, Salt Lake beyond capacity—and by that point, night would be just about finished worldwide anyway. Devaki said that pushing the issue in her community would have made people turn against the night sky, and that was not her purpose. So she went the other way with it, turning the association in a different direction, toward education and experiences, full moon snowshoe excursions, teaching school kids to take night sky measurements. She changed the name of the local alliance from "Dark Sky" to "Night Sky," because, she said, "dark" is false advertising. It can imply something dangerous or sinister. "What we're really after is night," she said. "When viewed in the right light, it's not entirely dark."

For the rancher with a sodium vapor bulb on a pole, she said, a successful outcome would not require them to do anything different. Instead, she'd let them know about motion sensors and downward-facing lights, directional lights, soft-colored LEDs. Success, for Devaki, is sending local ranchers to statewide or county programs allied with public utilities and non-profits like Ashley Pipkin's that can make it cheaper, maybe even free, to adjust their lighting. Perhaps someone like herself could come out and install shielding as a neighborly gesture. Success would be people deciding for themselves that the issue mattered, and that it was worth the work to preserve night skies in whatever way worked best for them. At that point, it would be done for the good of the sky.

I know a man living near me who for decades has been keeping track of lights he can see from his house. Bob McKeever lives on a rise that looks over our modest local population, and he's a night owl going to bed at one or two in the morning. He likes to sit in his outdoor hot tub before bed, which looks across ranch lands, and out of habit he counts the number of lights. To him it's like being on the edge of an enormous black sea. He and his town are the farthest lights out, nothing visible past us but pure darkness. For forty years he's been doing this counting from the hot tub. He first lived in the house he lives in now in 1985, and at the time he said there were twenty-three vapor lights that stayed on from sundown to morning. In the 2000s, he counted thirty-nine and he laughed to himself that the place was turning into a metro area.

Bob, who grew up in the area, told me in the 80s everybody had to have a mercury vapor fixture atop a pole or at the peak of a barn. "It was a status symbol," he said. "It was a must-have." Some people can't shake it. A couple who he called extreme preppers moved in from LA, and they lit their place like an armory. "When you live in a city, lights seem like security, but they really aren't," he said. He mentioned to the couple that their lights actually made their home more vulnerable, creating stark shadows where people can hide. They lead the eye straight to their place, giving away its general lay and location. Because of their radiance, he knew what they were up to and maybe they didn't want that. After the conversation, without anything else said, the lights came down.

In the 1970s, during the Cold War, Bob was in an artillery division of the Army stationed in Germany where his job was teaching soldiers how to use their own natural night vision. Positioned along the Czech border, he said life expectancy was eighteen minutes or less if conflict broke out. Soviet troops were directly across the border also operating under the cover of dark. This was before the widespread use of satellite surveillance and thermal imaging. He said lighting a cigarette was unacceptable, giving away your visual position and momentarily blotting night vision for you and anyone immediately nearby. He taught straight from the Army handbook how to use light from space through a tree canopy. These were mostly lessons in awareness. Biological human optics take thirty to forty-five minutes to adjust to the darkest places, and he'd demonstrate how a meager 15-watt bulb shined in your eyes for one second requires fifteen minutes for recovery. When you could die in eighteen minutes, that's precious time.

To this day, Bob prefers nighttime, the temperature, the feel of the air, and orienting himself using the moon and stars. What surprises him is that the trend of increasing light he's been watching for so long turned around as soon as people started talking about dark skies. Now by midnight he counts only six lights left on across the mesas, down from a high of thirty-nine. From his vantage in his hot tub, he knows who has decided to add to the darkness, and it's not only newcomers showing up with night sky ideals. "A lot of these are long-term residents," he said. "It's ranchers that have been here for quite a while. When I talk to them, personally, they really aren't on board with the dark sky concept. They've responded to it not because they're remodeling or an inspector says you can only have so many lumens. They're seeing what their neighbors are doing and they like it."

He told me people call him up and ask if he can see their lights from his house, and if he can see them that means many others can. Soon after that they go dark.

"I'm so proud," he said. "Sometimes you think people don't listen, but they actually do."

There are no lights tonight, no sign of anyone as far as the eye can see across the dark curve of the Earth. In the next basin over, City is experiencing this same bruised plumb of a sky. The earthwork's surface is decorated with geometric fins, pyramidal causeways, packed earth and smooth, bright concrete. Parts of it stand like great sundials. At night, they become nightdials. If there's any shadow at all, they'd show it. I'd been interested in taking measurements from City at night, and I reached out to the foundation which admits small numbers of visitors to explore the site on foot, the wait list a year long. I got back only autoresponders. That was wise of them. They wouldn't want us breaking City's black silence tonight.

This kind of dark is better viewed from the rim of a cattle tank. We sit on our little pads after dinner and watch nothing. Irvin says this is the kind of night he experienced while collecting insects in West Africa, where he experienced already dark skies blocked by jungle canopy. He tells me the guides, local Baka hunter-gatherers, would get up from the fire and file out of camp together without a word, barefoot and without lights, walking twelve miles back to the nearest village through heavy, untrailed growth. They would leave all at once, and you'd hear nothing in their departure as if they'd floated away.

I ask if they had the ground memorized, or if they could see where they were going. "I think they know how to feel through the dark," Irvin says. "They don't actually need trails. Certainly, just like anyone, they can develop trails, and they know how to get there. They have trees for landmarks, and they are aware of them in the dark."

We're learning to do evening tasks with as little lighting as possible, letting our hands guide us picking up and putting down gear, food, and water bottles. We're strengthening our proprioception, more aware of the spans of our bodies without having to see. It strikes me that Irvin and I have been in similar environmental conditions many times together, and I believe we've appreciated the experiences, but not like we are tonight. The act of paying attention makes the dark far more approachable.

Whatever sound I imagined emitted by our twenty-mile-long basin has gone away. Our breathing seems loud. I hear Irvin's lips when they part, when he's about to speak. What we both want to talk about is how quiet it is. It's a dilemma, for sure. Talking about how quiet it is makes it not quiet anymore. We finally sit and say nothing and the air cools another degree, smelling sweet, like water. Irvin feels a dab of rain on his shoulder and says something. I hear another strike my tent fly. A third hits ground, and a fourth.

"Okay," he says, and groans as he gets up. "It's time."

I do the same as the drops increase, and the ground begins shouting.

Rain comes on strong, roaring. I'm zipped into my space capsule where I can't see a thing, dark like the inside of a tomb. If the clouds had taken the night sky away, the tent doubles the sensation. Irvin's probably feeling the same, his nose not far from the tarp stretched taut above him. When the rain pauses, I shout for him, "How's it over there?"

"Snug!" he shouts back.

Knowing we are both tucked in, I close my eyes.

Never curse the rain. Sleep through it, wake, roll over, sleep again. This is why we set our camp on a cattle berm, higher than the surrounding terrain, if you can call anything terrain in this see-forever basin. If there is such a thing as a wasteland, we are in it.

I wake to dripping, but no rain, and unzip the inside mesh, then the outside fly, and crane myself out to look. It's not quite midnight. Mist from my breath rolls into the air, and my seeing it means there's light, brighter than when we fell asleep. Outer space is falling through windows between black-bottom clouds, revealing pockets and pools of stars.

For the rest of the night, between rains, sleeping and waking and unzipping the tent to see out, I put the puzzle together. The work is slow and dreamy, dragging my bag half out so I can position our eroded cattle tank amongst constellations, setting one compass atop another. As soon as the rain touches my cheeks and wakes me where I'd fallen asleep without noticing, I draw myself back in.

One in the morning, the storm has broken into big windows. Spaces between clouds glisten as if wet. In these drifting islands, stars are so numerous that in my half-awake state I feel vertigo, unable to orient myself until I find the "W" of Cassiopeia, which directs my eye to three points in the Big Dipper, and then to the North Star. Orion clears a shoulder. The seven sisters of the Pleiades are all there, framed in the middle of a black box; now far more than seven, more than I can count at once. Jupiter is high and so bright it obscures whatever's immediately around it. I fish out my binoculars and train them on the gas giant, picking out a couple pinpricks in a row, the planet's biggest moons.

Before the window moves away, I switch to the Pleiades, finding through lenses a den of young, brilliant, blue-white stars, a little crowd, estimated to be a thousand or more of them loosely bound by gravity. These stars formed together out of the same material around a hundred million years ago and have stuck together like ducklings.

When you hear that a person can see a few thousand stars in a single night sky, does that include clusters like the Pleiades? The Seven Sisters are the brightest seven of the cluster's thousand, held in wisps of gas and dust clouds called a *reflected nebula*, meaning the gas is lit from within by the many blue-white stars it contains. On the clearest night, like tonight, you can pick out strokes of molecular virga inside the Pleiades, a white haze the size of a dime held at arm's length. This small cosmic cloud is not stellar afterbirth from the Seven Sisters, which is what it looks like. Rather, this nomadic blanket of interstellar gas happens to be passing through the star cluster, illuminated as it goes by, a momentary collision. In thousands of years it will have moved on, fading into the inky backdrop, and the Pleiades will be piercingly bright and clear, no longer a nebula.

Binoculars go to my chest. Windows pass as slowly as whales. I try to stay awake, bag zipped to my face, and the stars unwind me back to sleep.

BORTLE 1

*   *   *   *   *   *   *   *   *   *   *

The presence of Jupiter or Venus in the sky seems to degrade dark adaptation. The zodiacal light, gegenschein, and zodiacal band are all visible—the zodiacal light to a striking degree, and the zodiacal band spans the entire sky. The galaxy M33 is an obvious naked-eye object even with direct vision. The Scorpius and Sagittarius regions of the Milky Way cast obvious diffuse shadows on the ground.

*   *   *   *   *   *   *   *   *   *   *

BORTLE 1

A
nn Finkbeiner, a science writer specializing in astronomy, particularly mapping the early universe, told me, "Every time I interview a scientist, I'm looking for why they're doing what they do. Astronomers really, really love astronomy. They really love their subjects. Almost more than any other science."

Finkbeiner, on the early side of her eighties, is an elder in the science-writing genre, and she still thinks the work of astronomers is a mystery. "I don't know what they're doing," she admitted. "I mean, I know what they're doing, but I have to take their word for it."

Other sciences are down here on Earth, immediate in all respects, a study of rocks and things that breathe. Space is far more expansive and out of reach, and it takes up most of reality even if we can't touch it. Finkbeiner sees the science as esoteric; it is, she said, a pure form of inquiry because it brings nothing but perspective. "Astronomy is so arcane it will never matter," she told me. "Don't say that to an astronomer, because they don't want to hear it. But it will never matter. It's very difficult what they do. And they are very, very smart people, very creative. So, I'd like to know what's worth burning up all those brain cells and creativity? What is it about astronomy that's worth these lives?"

For Finkbeiner, the fact-based study of the cosmos is an alternative to theology. She sees both as deriving from the same impulse for awe and elucidation. It's an attempt to arrange things and figure out what's happening.

I heard an alternate perspective from a college football player who ended up with a microphone at a National Football League scouting camp, and he said into it, "I don't believe in space."

He probably meant something else, I thought. How many stupid things have I said into microphones? I could have said that very thing.

"I don't think there's, like, other planets and stuff like that," he continued, with all seriousness and conviction.

Ok, he did mean it. This is not like Jim Enote from Zuni wondering what we're seeing up there, if stars could be people looking back at us. This is flat-out denial. The mind doesn't always take kindly to the thought of infinity. Countless nuclear engines swirling through galaxies as numberless as the stars can be a lot to take in, especially when going on faith. Who's actually been out there?

The young football player continued, "I'm real religious, so I think we're alone right now."

This means, if I may, that we are the only thing in the universe, which makes me think of Galileo standing trial before the Catholic Church in 1633 for saying that Earth was not the center of everything. The football player said he used to believe in the heliocentric universe, which Galileo proposed, but now he's finding that flat-earthers have valid points.

I took these statements to Richard Panek, one of Finkbeiner's astronomy-writing colleagues, and Panek's mouth struggled to come up with a response. He finally said, "It's a new one on me. It would never occur to me. It would be like saying the ocean isn't real. It makes no sense."

Panek has written books about gravity, dark matter, and the James Webb telescope. One of his early titles is *Seeing and Believing: A Short History of the Telescope and How We Look at the Universe.* Having eyeballed what's up there, he has trouble reconciling the notion of someone declaring space doesn't exist.

"Where do you..." he searched. "Where do you begin?"

I suggested that not believing could be a reaction to the feeling of insignificance we so often face in the presence of immeasurable grandeur. It's why we call it the heavens, being so much more than a person can grasp.

Panek said, "If you need the universe to tell you that you're insignificant, you haven't been paying attention."

I took the football player's perspective to Finkbeiner for a second opinion. She thought for a moment, then said, "Well, in a way, it's kind of reasonable."

Reasonable was not what I expected from an accomplished writer in astronomical disciplines. Of all people, she knows space is real.

"I grew up in the country," she explained. "I didn't get really interested in astronomy until I was in my early forties, but when I was a kid, I spent a lot of time looking at the night sky. It wouldn't have occurred to me that the moon didn't go across the sky. It wouldn't have occurred to me that the sun didn't go across the sky. It would never have occurred to me that the stars were up there during the day. If I'd been pushed, I would have thought that everything up in the sky is pretty much the same distance from us."

A plastic sky, a constructed model, a place right above the highest clouds. If you never learned what we know about space, or if you won't believe what we've learned, that's precisely what it would look like, a child's-eye view. The sky would seem flat. Finkbeiner reminded me that the only reason I know that a particular blood-red dot is Mars is because someone told me, there was data, photos coming back from landers, and I believed them. I saw images and learned about the planet's circumference and age, its whopper-jawed moons, the finding of water in both ice and liquid form, and all that became part of my knowledge. Something 150 million miles away was made more factual and tangible.

"You believe what you can see, right?" Finkbeiner said.

She told me about waking up to view a solar eclipse early in the morning and she got the timing wrong. The eclipse wasn't happening when she went outside. "They must have rescheduled it, or it must be delayed," she said. "That was my first thought."

She knew better, of course, but living in this civilization, we get used to humans being in charge.

"What age was that?" I asked.

"It wasn't that long ago," she said.

For Finkbeiner, space can be subjective; it depends on your mood, what you believe or don't, and most of it is out of reach, so who's the wiser? She said, "It's not unreasonable to say I believe only what I can observe and what my experience has been."

My experience of the cosmos comes from an early age, and I am past the point of imagining anything other than an infinite expanse of physical galaxies and stars beyond our planets. Growing up in the country and becoming a science writer, Finkbeiner would say the same. Panek lives in Manhattan, and he's seen what's up there in intimate detail through telescopes of all shapes and sizes. The football player, I don't know. Maybe he never got on those high school programs with Irvin and me and he never saw a richly appointed night sky. We each have a unique relationship with what we see up there, and I'm firmly on the side of Finkbeiner and Panek who see space as nothing but real. As real as clouds, as real as Earth. It is an act of faith to extrapolate across such distances, believing in Mars and in giant stars hanging in the fabric of galactic arms. It is an act of science to show us what we can't see.

Finkbeiner said, "You know, for the early Christians curiosity was a sin."

"There's a whole universe that is really none of our business," I said.

"But I want to know," she said.

—

I throw back a wet tent flap and slouch into dawn. The air smells like a cold herbarium; it's the end of the season, knee-high drought-tolerant bushes giving up their last fetid sugars. The basin is a wet expanse of autumnal saltbush and greasewood, swollen sponge-clay, and clouds that seem to want to be on the ground rather than in the air. I can see for many miles and there is no standing water. The night's rain, on the verge of snow, got soaked up. I walk the ring of the Bortle Hole looking for a place to pee, which is anywhere on the rim of this old, earthen cattle tank. The ground drinks it.

Morning sounds like clouds pulling away from each other, the sound of soft bread being torn open. The planet's turn is slow, and weather parts for it, sun finding its way through shreds of leftover storm, sending god-fingers of morning light across the basin. None of the rays quite reach us. Irvin's trying to get a fire going, stripping dead, calcified shrub wood to reach the dry material inside, and his efforts produce mostly smoke on this gray, gloomy, electrified morning. He blows and blows until a flame sparks up and climbs through his stack of kindling. Now we have a place to stand and warm our hands.

We have little need to talk, except to comment about our bodies finally not seeming damaged. It's the first morning I haven't felt like my thighs were peeling from bone. Of course, it's our last day. He says he could go another thousand miles, and his saying it makes me think of the dark in the Alvord Desert north of here in Oregon, or the Atacama five thousand miles south. That's where we should be going from here. Why are we stopping? Promises to keep, I suppose. A ride like that would take us in and out of Bortles, some of the darkest places we've been, some of the brightest. We'd have to get out to sea, a thousand miles from any lightbulb dangling above a door drawing moths, and with the proper data set, we could compare and contrast one kind of dark from another. This is someone's lifetime calling. Irvin calls what we're doing Bortle-hopping, moving from one dark zone to the next. I tell him

I like the biking routine, the daily rituals, and the speed of travel. The pace has been just right to see the change. Already we are congratulating each other when we have one night left, our Hail Mary about to take us across this basin.

The road is well-graveled, not swampy, and our smoke will reveal our location when our friends show up in their 1985 VW van. When they ramble into the basin that morning, we can hear the engine whine for miles, their van decked out as if for a moon voyage. They're a husband and wife team and they've been camping in the area, moving from one range to the next. Their van is our ride back to Vegas. When they show up and park along the road, we meet with big hugs.

The day becomes a grand and ragged ballet of mountains cutting through clouds as broad and flat-bellied as manta rays. I've missed clouds. A blank desert sky needs gilding now and then. The road hums under my tires as sunlight reaches the road. Irvin's a mile ahead—though distance here is easy to lose track of, maybe two or three miles. We've sent the van on so we can finish our last day on the bikes. We'll go as far as we can across this basin and put the urban glow behind us, meeting to camp tonight.

My rear tire gradually softens, a repair on a flat—one of three so far—not quite holding. I stop, pull out our little pump, attach it to the stem, and start working. As I pump, my head lifts to watch the show. The mountains are decorated with shards of sunlight, and the basin, which is drier and warmer than the surrounding high country, has put a clear hole in the sky. Clouds curve around the edges, mirroring the basin's length and width. Earth and sky look like a circus, everything whirling and balancing, a whole different act than the invocation of night. The air is rarified, smelling like a freshly minted coin. Near the horizon, the atmosphere is Bahama blue, an ocean lagoon, while overhead it's closer to the black of space, a blue so deep you think you're seeing through it.

Today is all about the night still to come. Most of our gear has been switched to the van and miles pass with ease. The road is puddled but mostly dry, the sun's warmth strong on our backs and on the ground. The closest we get to the City installation is a couple of miles. Leaving bikes behind, we climb a rocky-headed knoll to see Heizer's strange, motionless metropolis in the distance. The massive art installation doesn't seem like much from here, a shiny cluster of what looks like abandoned runways with cloud shadows drifting across them. What is more interesting is a dead rattlesnake we find partly eaten and mummified atop the knoll, probably dropped by a raptor, maybe a fight to the death up here. Irvin gingerly holds up the crisp body, bringing its face to his nose for a sniff. "I think I can smell the fang," he says.

We return to our bikes and pedal onward, leaving the knoll and City behind for the far side of our basin. Mountain shadows march across stiff, knee-high brush that stretches as far as one can see. Ranges tip this way and that like a tectonic naval battle, some of the ships halfway sunk, some still afloat. Clouds leftover from yesterday hug the ranges, and the sky over us yawns wide. This, I think, promises to be an extraordinary night.

We catch up with our friends in the sunset shadow of a mountain, and the van is pulled over, table set up. High fives and hugs—the husband is the guy who hired Irvin and me to guide for the company decades ago, the reason we know each other. His wife is a sleek bike rider that he couldn't keep up with if he tried. They've brought a feast, our own little Vegas buffet of cheeses, meats, crackers, and dinner kindly prepared in a cook set on a propane stove. As evening sets in, Irvin and I have one request: one last dark camp, no white lights, and, as fairy-like and pleasant as they are, no strings of holiday lights around the van. The request is met with a huzzah, a toast, and whiskey in our jars. Welcome to Bortle 1.

The deepest night I've seen was in the Atacama, a high-elevation desert with cool air coming clean off the South Pacific onto the

Chilean coast. This is where the largest Earth-based telescopes are erected, offering as good a view into space as is possible without going there. I traveled on foot with a friend in this desert, dropped off far from lights. Carrying with us all the water we needed, we walked for several days. The nearest city, Antofagasta, 440,000 people, was on the coast 130 miles away, and none of its light reached this far.

The Magellanic Clouds were not just cotton balls. We could see shapes of disks inside of them, giving them away as two irregular dwarf galaxies floating just outside our galaxy two hundred thousand light-years away. The Southern Hemisphere is noticeably more brilliant than its northern counterpart, its Milky Way containing more color variations, stars more numerous. The southern half of the planet looks toward our galactic core with its greater concentrations of stars. From the Atacama, Zodiacal light formed a band across the sky as if the Earth had a dusty ring around it. In this light, our shadows played against the ground. We lay on our backs and watched the glitter of tiny shooting stars as interplanetary sand grains collided with the atmosphere. The Milky Way was impenetrable, molten at its center, marked with lanes of gas clouds darker than any shade of black. The sky was not dark; it was the opposite of dark, a sky suffused with light. As we lay there, my friend began talking about navigation, piloting a sailboat, and I could picture its keel splitting the stars overhead, the boat's wake rippling as if through a bioluminescent sea.

Back at home in Colorado, I spoke with a filmmaker who lives nearby and had recently returned from a gig in the Atacama where he spent a month and a half filming night skies for a movie. He confided that, seen through the camera, our Colorado skies are better than the famously clear atmosphere of one of the driest deserts in the world. In the high, northern Chilean sky, he noticed a persistent and almost invisible band of moisture—something up in the stratosphere that must drive telescope operators mad. He said it's nothing I would have seen when I was there, even with binoculars, but through stacks of lenses and time-lapses he picked up a reddish hue from airglow, stray sunlight, and the faraway twinge of heavy metal mining operations. He said where we are in the West, you get a clearer picture. At home, we have one of the best astronomical views he's ever seen.

I walk among the shadow-shapes of dryland bushes as voices trail behind me, glasses clinking, bottles uncorking. I don't have to look up to see the sky, it's everywhere above my shoulders. The stages of dusk have ended and the weight of night has arrived. If the sky were music, it would be Beethoven at the height of madness, mopped in sweat and conducting the universe. We are two hundred miles by bike from Vegas, one hundred thirty miles as the crow flies, and it feels like the stars might buzz out of their skin.

Enough with the satellites already. Now it's becoming absurd, nowhere to look without seeing little fairy seeds moving left and right. This advent is what might most puzzle the ancients. Try explaining this development, how we've made what look like stars that move swiftly and seemingly at will. I've been witness to Starlink launches over the past few years as they've gone from mesmerizing to irritating, leaving us on the ground wondering who has the right to reorder the heavens with trains of low-orbit satellites going up on each other's heels? Currently, one of the brightest artificial objects in the sky, second to the International Space Station, is the BlueWalker 3 cell phone satellite with a reflective antenna the size of a billboard, and it is a prototype with hundreds more to come. Ten thousand satellites are in orbit right now and fifty thousand are expected by the end of the decade. I was glad to see their whimsical trails when they first started to appear several nights ago, and I waved at them like we must have waved at Sputnik in 1957, but this is overwhelming. We are taking over of the sky.

After a quarter mile, I can still hear my friends, and I'm grateful for the sounds I've been missing, conversations I'm not part of. My footsteps are clear in my ears, and I wear the same dusty pants I've been wearing since Vegas, sweeping past rabbitbrush and the scrape of blackbrush. Voices magnify the silence, giving it parameters, a solitary ping in the wilderness. We are the only human thing happening out here, and our mingled sounds make it somehow quieter.

The van's soft glow in the distance supplies my eye with something to triangulate off of, giving the map in my head a geodetic quality. If the van is over there and I am over here, the stars must be very, very far away. A moon sharp and slender as the edge of a clamshell rides low in the west. It's tipped on its side, freshly back from its newness, a sliver of honey milk bright enough to put a glow on my open hands. Most of the moon is shaded, but visible with ephemeral, umbral moonshine. That's the Earth lighting up the dark side of the moon, sunshine bounced twice, enough to make out larger craters and basaltic maria. The last moon I saw was from Sphere in the Bortle 9, a crescent piggybacking Venus through a lens of light pollution. Back then, the moon, the real one in space, was the most apparent thing to see, while tonight it is one gleaming edge of jewelry in an overflowing chest of gems and silver pieces. It stands out, but you could lose it.

On the clock of the night sky, the moon is the little hand. The sun is the big hand turning the hours, while the moon counts out the more intricate movements. The stars are the face of the clock and they, too, turn. When it sets, the moon's horns drop behind a range, and the night turns up a notch. Now it is the mighty face of the clock alone. This is the light of a pure and moonless sky. Clouds have parted for the entire presentation, and the North Star is bright enough to really matter. I've been counting what shows of the Seven Sisters of the Pleiades since night one, and now I see far more than seven in this misty little cluster. It looks like a shattered diamond.

In Cherokee, Iroquois, and early Greek astronomy, this aster-ism is called Seven Sisters, and to the Tuareg Berbers of the north-ern Sahara it is Cat ahăḍ, "daughters of the night." I agree there's something feminine and related about this dense little cluster. Over thousands of years its stars have drifted in relation to each other, and two of the brightest have moved into each other's paths till they look like one, which might be why it is still called Seven Sis-ters, instead of the six we can usually see. I like that telling, but tonight I don't think it's the case. You see six main stars and the seventh is the other thousand giving this passing gas cloud its glow. It makes you think you're seeing far more than six. There are so many sisters your eye could never find them all.

Constellations seem to have vanished, Orion a challenge to draw from its glimmering bed, no longer the bold hunter but a celestial swimmer. The Big Dipper wheels around a triple-star sys-tem that looks like one, Polaris. Andromeda and the Orion Nebula lie in their beds of fleece. It all got thrown up there just like that, everything in place the way Coyote meant it.

The Milky Way is dancing, showing off. It has topography. Two billion of its suns have been mapped, estimated to be one percent of the total number in the disk alone, giving my galactic view a milky haze. My habit is to untangle the heavens, locating us within the inner rim of the Orion Arm of the Milky Way Galaxy, positioned inside the Virgo Galactic Supercluster, which belongs to the Pisces-Cetus Supercluster. Usually it's work to forget, but not tonight, my eye a simple organ that only sees light and some of the colors that come with it. Even with limited human vision, the sky is overflowing. Everything looks like a constellation, a palimpsest of arrangements—triangles, half-circles, parallelograms. It no longer matters which way is which.

The mountains are black, bereft of light, causing the sky to blaze and the Milky Way to wave like a banner. The galactic struc-ture is now well defined, with stellar concentrations glowing and streamers of gas clouds blocking the light. Galactic archaeologists would look at this ancient swath of light like studying a fossil, peering into its foramina and sockets, understanding how the beast of our galaxy moves and evolves. This is what Jenny Ouyang saw for the first time and cried, not just a scattershot of thousands of stars, but a shimmering bridge spanning from one side of the sky to the other.

My mentor in college was J. McKim Malville, who at the time was chair of the Department of Astrogeophysics at University of Colorado in Boulder. Kim, as he's known, helped keep my interest in night skies going, loading me up with books and papers on cosmology, sending me down rabbit holes of collective creation myths, introducing me to the science of chaos theory. In an exchange about qualities of dark and light in the night sky, Kim recently wrote to me, "There's some irony in how terribly hard it is to find darkness in our universe. There's no darkness, for instance, in a cloud of dark matter. But there's no better place to hide from light than inside those dark globules of dust, such as in the Pillars of Creation in the Eagle Nebula, out of which light, live stars, and life itself eventually emerge."

This is a sky I can no longer call dark. By the metric of my eye, it is full of light. Knowing this will be the brightest night of the trip, bright without human lighting, I walk until voices fade, putting myself out in it. I'm up to my neck in stars, in what Kim Malville reinforced in me as a menagerie of mythic, astronomical structures and possibilities, not just the void of space. The sensation of seeing it with your own eyes is akin to plunging your body into cold water, a sweeping rearrangement of what you understood the world to be by daylight. Zest enters the blood and skin tingles. That you can't physically feel the night's weight is astonishing, a teaspoon of a neutron star coming in at ten million tons, a sheer gas cloud several hundred light-years across knotting itself with enough mass to collapse into millions of suns. You should feel this on your shoulders. It should be singing with a beautiful voice. It lifts you off the ground.

Standing in this basin with dew gathering on my shoulders and on my jacket hood, I can't say I hear the music of the spheres the way some ancient Greeks claimed they could. I'm holding up my light meter and my ears have a bit of a ring, but that might be me wanting to hear it. I'm unsure if I heard these celestial tones when I was a kid, if my dad heard them, or whether Pythagoras or Ptolemy did. I believe it is not a sound that can be listened to, but rather it's the brain filling a sensory blank. With so much going on, there must be some kind of racket.

My final reading is 21.8, which I count as a touchdown under a clear sky, reaching the ball over the line and planting it at the Bortle 1 line. I search until I find the bump of Las Vegas as faint as one of the visible nebulas, ineffectual against the greater skyscape. From this far out, it is next to nothing. Holding my thumb at arm's length, I extinguish it. The light of the city where we started is finally gone.

Every hour or two I wake long enough to see what's happening in the sky before drifting off again. The radiance is enough to cast a shadow as if by a slender moon, only there's no moon. I can see the gegenschein light, which consists of dust particles congregating around the gravitational alignment of the sun and Earth. It is a faint, diffuse arc that shines opposite the sun, a point out on the ecliptic denser with interplanetary dust than anywhere else. Sunlight traveling through deep space bounces back from it as if from a diaphanous mirror.

The last dark stretch brings Venus, and Venus brings the first astronomical twilight, then the nautical cladding of morning. I'm seeing dawn light lasting longer and more colorfully because my eye has adjusted, and because in this farther country it shows itself more vividly. This side of twilight looks much more like Steinbeck's "hour of pearl" than it did at the edge of Vegas. Every moment turns a new kind of blue. I believe this is what Steinbeck meant when he wrote that time stops and examines itself at this time of day. At the peak of this drawn-out interlude, daytime and night hang in the balance for so long one could forget which is which.

Nine in the morning, steam comes off of me in direct daylight. We're slow to move, a bottle of whiskey and one of red wine drained last night and left out. A crunch of frost lies across anything we didn't cover or put away, our panniers and bikes, the table with its dishes washed and turned over. Coffee is available through the van door, but I'm not a coffee drinker. Instead, I walk out of camp, away from the van, and I keep walking around one dryland bush after the next. Covering ground without a bike is unfamiliar. My body remembers itself in a different way. Every few minutes I stop to hold out an arm, framing an angle of sky with thumb and forefinger until I find the little gem of Venus. My eyesight hasn't been improving, nothing about rods and cones getting better. I have simply been more aware, able to consciously bump sightings till later each morning. I used to lose it at sunrise and now it's a couple hours past and I'm still finding its pinprick.

Limestone as tough and sharp as teeth rises layer by layer into mountains. Citadels of gray rock lead higher, one ramping, fossilized sea floor after the next. The van shrinks below me, becoming smaller each time I look. I can see smoke; Irvin is starting his morning fire out of last night's coals.

The limestone is loaded with caves and declivities clawed at by erosion and sprinkled with tiny marine fossils, signs of life from an ancient planet. I follow my shadow into a rough natural shelter that faces east, a closet-sized space that gathers the morning's warmth. Crouching in the back, I feel like a statue or an offering for the sun in a mountainous niche. This is how we began—so long ago it's beyond conscious memory—crouching in our shelters to keep the sky inside ourselves, figuring out where we needed to be for first light, marking shadows and learning where the daylight would go next. From the start, we paid attention to risings and settings, the cave mouth framing a golden sun, a stubbled, honey-colored basin below, edges skimmed in fog from the last rain. The van is a white dot, its own little Venus on the ground.

I search the blue and one last time find the glint of our sister planet, a bit of night sky to tuck into my pocket for the day.

FORMULA 1

The firefighter who loaned us the bikes is working the Grand Prix in Vegas. He's captain of the extraction crew; when necessary, he pulls drivers out of twisted wrecks or rescues people who find themselves in a hazardous pinch.

The first night of the big race is the first night we're back in town from our ride, and Erik Klausen—former mountain bike guide and father of two—can't join us because he's working the race. Irvin whips up a feast in the hotel studio where we're camped. He cooks hot-spiced squid and dishes with salted duck eggs, fish flakes, and heaps of vegetables we picked up at a Filipino supermarket in the city. From the hotel balcony after dinner, we marvel at the shimmer of Vegas and how it ends at sharp boundaries, with nothing past it but darkness. I plotted our trip so we could follow one basin after the next, as few mountains as possible to block our line of sight from the city. Like a slingshot, we snapped back, standing now on a balcony listening to the ass-clinching scream of race cars a couple miles away.

In the center of Vegas, Erik is parked on the side of the track in a sleek white pickup with the word EXTRACTION blazed across its hood. It's two or three in the morning and racing is over for the night. One of the cars, worth tens of millions of dollars, sucked a manhole cover clean out of the street and crashed it through the vehicle's tender undercarriage. No one was injured, but for the car, and the damaged raceway has to be resurfaced overnight, every manhole cover paved over to prevent a repeat. Erik is required to stay until repaving is done.

He's on the job with nothing to do, no sleeping allowed as steampunk paving machines groan and smoke, rolling dense, smooth asphalt at a turtle's pace. There's only so long a person can sit in the front seat of an extraction vehicle listening to silence on the radio and watching pavers. He moves to the truck bed, hands laced behind his head, and lies on his back looking up.

From the bed, gear pushed out of the way, he counts five stars—no, four stars and one is a planet. It's not much, but it's something. He and his family live in a small, funky desert community outside the city, population less than three hundred, and it's blessed with a mountain range that blocks direct light from Vegas. Despite being so close to the blazing nucleus, they've got a decent sky. He goes with his family out farther to camp, and their young kids are growing up acquainted with places where you can see the whole universe; you look up and there it is, a birthright. Wherever their kids go from here, they can speak to childhood skies, how it felt like you could reach up and touch the stars.

On the racetrack, Erik is looking into one of the brightest skies on Earth, light that shows every pore on his face. He counts again, finding no more, no less, four stars and a planet, a place for the night sky to begin.

About the Author

CRAIG CHILDS is an explorer who brings tales of deserts and ice caps to the page. He has published more than a dozen critically acclaimed books, including *The Secret Knowledge of Water*, *Atlas of a Lost World*, *Stone Desert*, *Virga & Bone*, and *Tracing Time*. His books have won numerous honors including the Reading the West Book Award, Southwest Book of the Year, a Foreword INDIES medal, and the Orion Book Award. His nonfiction narratives and journalism have appeared in *The Atlantic*, *Outside*, *High Country News*, *The New York Times*, *The Sun*, the *Los Angeles Times*, NPR, and Radiolab. Childs lives in southwest Colorado.

About the Cover Artist

JEREMY COLLINS is known for his complex, cerebral, and whimsical drawings and maps featured in his books, films, and commercial work. From the cover of *National Geographic* to his own company, Meridian Line, he is a driving force within and beyond the Outdoor Industry Association, who awarded him "Most Inspirational Individual."

As an activist, Collins has donated his time, voice, and work to causes he believes in for many years. He has hand delivered art to the Senate floor in Utah to fight for protection of Bears Ears National Monument, travelled by river in the Arctic National Wildlife Refuge with the Sierra Club to tell stories for its protection, and shared his powerful street and activism art around the US. His work supports numerous environmental programs, and he produces an annual wall calendar of his art that provides activism initiatives to inspire us all to do better. Collins lives in Running Springs, California.

About Torrey House Press

Torrey House Press publishes books at the intersection of the literary arts and environmental advocacy. THP authors explore the diversity of human experiences and relationships with place. THP books create conversations about issues that concern the American West, landscape, literature, and the future of our ever-changing planet, inspiring action toward a more just world.

We believe that lively, contemporary literature is at the cutting edge of social change. We seek to inform, expand, and reshape the dialogue on environmental justice and stewardship for the natural world by elevating literary excellence from diverse voices.

Visit www.torreyhouse.org for reading group discussion guides, author interviews, and more.

As a 501(c)(3) nonprofit publisher, our work is made possible by generous donations from readers like you.

This book was made possible by the generous support of Susan Markley. Torrey House Press is supported by Back of Beyond Books, Bright Side Bookshop, The King's English Bookshop, Maria's Bookshop, the Ballantine Family Fund, the Jeffrey S. & Helen H. Cardon Foundation, the Lawrence T. Dee & Janet T. Dee Foundation, the McMullan/O'Connor Family Fund, the Stewart Family Foundation, the Barker Foundation, Kif Augustine & Stirling Adams, Diana Allison, Richard Baker, Karey Barker, Patti Baynham & Owen Baynham, Matt Bean, Klaus Bielefeldt, Joe Breddan, Karen Buchi & Kenneth Buchi, Betty Clark & Gary Clark, Rose Chilcoat & Mark Franklin, Linc Cornell & Lois Cornell, Susan Cushman & Charlie Quimby, Lynn de Freitas & Patrick de Freitas, Pert Eilers, Ed Erwin, Laurie Hilyer, Phyllis Hockett, Kirtly Parker Jones, Emily Klass, Rick Klass, Jen Lawton & John Thomas, Susan Markley, Leigh Meigs & Stephen Meigs, Mark Meloy, Kathleen Metcalf, Donaree Neville & Douglas Neville, Laura Paskus, Katie Pearce, Marion S. Robinson, Molly Swonger, Shelby Tisdale, Rachel White, the National Endowment for the Humanities, the National Endowment for the Arts, the Utah Division of Arts & Museums, Utah Humanities, the Salt Lake City Arts Council, and Salt Lake County Zoo, Arts & Parks. Our thanks to individual donors, members, and the Torrey House Press board of directors for their valued support.

Join the Torrey House Press community and give today at www.torreyhouse.org/give.